The NATIONAL PARKS of America

The Editors of Country Beautiful • Editorial Direction: Michael P. Dineen
Edited by Robert L. Polley • Managing Editor: Charles R. Fowler
Contributing Editors: Joseph Dever, Frank Sullivan, William Bibber

The NATIONAL

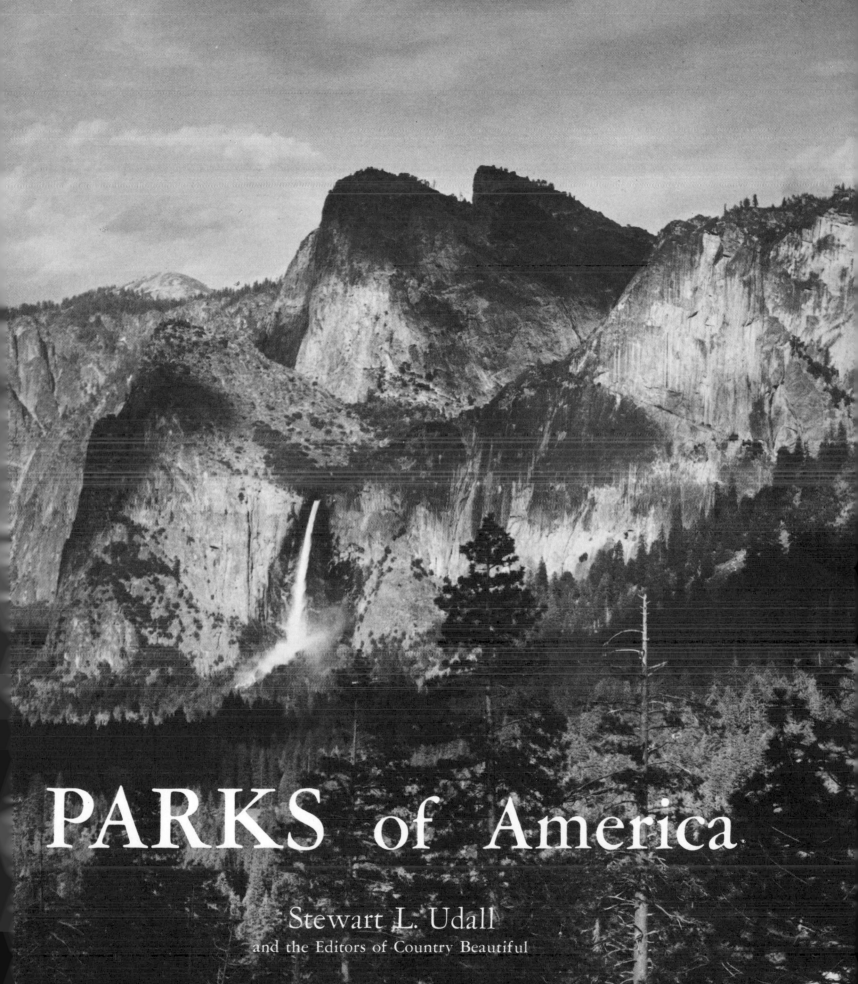

PARKS of America

Stewart L. Udall
and the Editors of Country Beautiful

Published by G. P. Putnam's Sons, New York
In association with Country Beautiful Foundation, Inc., Waukesha, Wisconsin

COUNTRY BEAUTIFUL: *Publisher and Editorial Director:* Michael P. Dineen; *Executive Editor:* Robert L. Polley; *Managing Editor:* Charles R. Fowler; *Contributing Editors:* Joseph Dever, Frank Sullivan, William Bibber; *Senior Editors:* Kenneth L. Schmitz, James H. Robb; *Assistant Art Director:* Robert Fehring; *Editorial Assistant:* Joseph M. Treen; *Distribution:* Bernard J. Connell, Mel Rozier, John Dineen; *Design and Technical Consultant:* Robert W. Pradt; *Administration:* B. Robert Peck; *Assistants:* Sharon G. Armao, Vicki R. Kurovsky, Trudy Schnittka, Kathleen Kons.

COUNTRY BEAUTIFUL Magazine is published by Country Beautiful Foundation, Inc., 24198 W. Bluemound Road, Waukesha, Wis. 53186, a nonprofit organization dedicated to strengthening and preserving the physical, cultural and moral values of America and other nations of the world.

PHOTO CREDITS

Backleaf (full title page): El Capitan (left), Half Dome (rear center) and Bridalveil Fall (right) are preserved at Yosemite, one of the 32 national parks.

CONTENTS

INTRODUCTION

THE BEAUTY AND WONDER OF THE AMERICAN EARTH

At Cape Lookout on the magnificent outer banks of North Carolina, I watched a sea gull beat its lonely way against a sudden rainstorm that lashed the Atlantic shore. Leaning into the wind, the taste of the salt spray on my lips, I walked for miles along this isolated stretch of sand and dunes, soothed by the roar of crashing waves.

Only a few weeks before, President Johnson had signed legislation passed by the 89th Congress authorizing the establishment of this beautiful 58-mile barrier beach as the Cape Lookout National Seashore. Now, children of all generations would be assured of a place to watch sea gulls and sanderlings chase the waves — or see great flights of migratory birds take refuge in salt marshes along the Atlantic flyway — or build their world of tomorrow on the white sands of a timeless shore.

Here was tangible evidence of continuing conservation success under the dynamic leadership of a park-minded President who said that:

> If future generations are to remember us more with gratitude than with sorrow, we must achieve more than just the miracles of technology. We must also leave them a glimpse of the world as God really made it, not just as it looked when we got through with it.

It is in the spirit of this message that the National Park Service, in 1966, celebrated its 50th Anniversary. Its half-century of public service has been dedicated to

The proposed Voyageurs National Park, Minnesota.

the principle of protecting and administering this nation's most superlative areas of scenic grandeur, scientific wonder and historic significance for the use and enjoyment of the American people for all time.

Who can trace the genesis of "the national park idea"? Many believe it was born in the year 1864 when President Lincoln signed the act transferring the beautiful Yosemite Valley and Mariposa Grove of Big Trees to the State of California ". . . for public use, resort and recreation." But the "idea" certainly gained its fullest recognition in the Act of 1872 establishing Yellowstone National Park — the first of its kind in the world. In this act, the Congress spelled out a new public land policy — that the scenic masterpieces of the public domain were to be dedicated and set apart in perpetuity — not for material gain or riches — but, rather, for the benefit and enjoyment of all the people "as a public park or pleasuring ground."

The original national park concept was concerned primarily with natural features and scenic resources. But in the years after 1900, vandalism and indiscriminate looting of prehistoric Indian sites in the Southwest resulted in the passage of the Antiquities Act of 1906. This act extended the public land policy to provide authority for the President, by proclamation, to set aside as national monuments, " . . .Historic landmarks and prehistoric structures, and other objects of historic or scientific interest that are situated upon the lands owned or controlled by the Government of the United

9

States . . . ." This legal machinery enabled Theodore Roosevelt and other Presidents to preserve such diverse areas as the Grand Canyon, Petrified Forest, Casa Grande, Saguaro and the Organ Pipe Cactus.

A half-century ago, America's growing collection of national parks and monuments was loosely administered by several diverse agencies of the Federal Government. National parks were administered by the Secretary of the Interior, but patrolled by soldiers detailed by the Secretary of War — much in the manner of forts and garrisons. This was necessary, of course, in those early days of the "wild and woolly West" when highwaymen actually held up coaches and robbed visitors to Yellowstone National Park, and game poachers operated freely within park boundaries.

National monuments, too, were administered in various ways. Under the Antiquities Act of 1906, monuments of military significance were turned over to the Secretary of War, and, following the same "logic," monuments within or adjacent to national forests were placed under the Department of Agriculture. The rest, and greatest number, were placed under the jurisdiction of the Department of the Interior, with each park superintendent reporting directly to the Secretary, who had little time to coordinate the management of parklands.

By this time, John Muir — the indomitable "John of the Mountains" — had played a vital role in establishing six of the nation's superb national parks — Sequoia, Yosemite, Mount Rainier, Crater Lake, Glacier and Mesa Verde — and a dozen parklike national monuments, including two that eventually became national parks, Grand Canyon and Olympic.

Among the most inspired by Muir was Stephen Tyng Mather, of 20 Mule Team Borax fame, a Chicago businessman whose love for the out-of-doors brought about his chance meeting with Muir in 1912. Two years later — indignant over land depredations in Sequoia and Yosemite, and appalled at the sight of cattle grazing inside the parks — Mather wrote an irate letter to Secretary of the Interior, Franklin K. Lane. He complained that the parks were underfinanced, mismanaged, without decent roads and accommodations and a disgrace to the Federal Government. Lane replied: "Dear Steve: If you don't like the way the national parks are being run, come on down to Washington and run them yourself."

Mather arrived on the scene when the use of the automobile was just gaining popularity, and at a time when American neutrality discouraged travel in war-torn Europe. Attention of both wealthy and average-income Americans turned quite naturally to the beauties and attractions of their own country, and the dirt roads of Yellowstone and Yosemite were choked with dust. But if public interest in the national parks was on the rise, it was not matched by the interest of the Congress. As Chairman of the House Appropriations Committee from 1897 to 1903, and Speaker of the House from 1903 to 1911, "Uncle Joe" Cannon stuck pretty close to his expressed philosophy: "Not one cent for scenery!" When asked for money to run the parks, some Congressman retorted that the nation should "get out of the show business," and "quit raising wild animals." "The best thing the Government could do with Yellowstone National Park," one of them said, "is to survey it and sell it." But time has wrought changes, and today Congress often leads the people in the establishment of parks.

The year 1966, the Golden Anniversary of the National Park Service, was also a salute to Mather whose dedication to the cause of conservation brought about the Historic Act of 1916 which created the National Park Service and gave it the mission to "promote and regulate the use of . . . national parks, monuments . . . ." in order:

> . . . to conserve the scenery and the natural and historic objects and the wild life therein and to provide for the enjoyment of same in such manner and by such means as will leave them unimpaired for future generations.

When Steve Mather joined the Department of the Interior in 1915, there were 14 maladministered national parks and 18 national monuments. By the time failing health forced him to resign in 1929, there were 41 superb units under one creative plan of management.

He laid the foundations of the National Park Service, defining and establishing the policies under which its areas shall be developed and conserved so that the "national park idea" remains today a conservation ideal in all parts of the world. It has been well said of Steve Mather: ". . . There will never come an end to the good that he has done."

Strangely enough, one of Mather's chief concerns in those days was to get people to visit the parks. In persuading one investor to build a hotel in Yosemite Valley — a sober man who drew back in fear of empty rooms and little business — Mather said: "Why, look at those cars! There must be 200. Where's your imagination, man? Some day there'll be a thousand!" In 1965, hundreds of thousands of cars brought 1,635,400 visitors to Yosemite National Park. On one Memorial Day weekend, alone, there were over 49,000 visitors, and 35,000 of these spread their tents and parked their camping vehicles in the beautiful Yosemite Valley. So the change has come and with it a new problem: How can the parks be managed for the pleasure of the people without destruction of the values which give them pleasure?

A decade ago, neglect again threatened our parks, following years of austerity during the great depression and during and immediately following World War II and the Korean conflict. Even more significant than this temporary limitation of funds for park purposes, however, was the phenomenal postwar demand for outdoor recreation and the unexpected increase in park use by the American public. In 1941, at the time of Pearl Harbor, there had been only 21 million visits recorded to national parks and monuments. This jumped to 50 million in 1955. With the improvement of air travel, with each mile of improved road and with each year's new automobile models, America's vacation horizons were expanding and our travel and recreation habits continued to change. The physical plant of the National Park System, developed in the early 1930's, was becoming rapidly obsolete.

In 1956, Director Conrad L. Wirth launched *Mission 66* — a ten-year program of modernization and expansion to provide more adequate accommodations for vacationers, and to construct visitor centers, picnic areas, campgrounds and trails in keeping with the magnificent surroundings of natural beauty. Then, it was predicted that visits to areas of the National Park System by 1966 would total 80 million, a figure so startling that some believed it unreasonable. That mark is behind us; there were 137 million visits during the 50th Anniversary Year.

Mission 66 has been an amazingly effective program, and it is a tribute to Connie Wirth, to his successor, George B. Hartzog, Jr., and to all those others responsible for its success.

Today, there are over 231 areas within the system — encompassing some 27 million acres of the finest parklands in the world. Each park has its unique story to tell, its own rewards to offer. Each contributes to a deeper understanding and appreciation of the history of the United States and of our way of life; of the natural processes which have given form to our land, and of the environment in which we live and of which we are a part.

Back in the most discouraging days of neglect, Bernard de Voto, a staunch friend of the national parks, said "If we cannot protect the parks and decently care for visitors, let us close the parks." Today, we are faced with a spiraling increase of attendance that makes us all wonder what to do — except, perhaps, for those lucky superintendents of Isle Royale, the Virgin Islands, Mount McKinley and a few other hard-to-get-to parks. The situation aggravates the perennial built-in problem: How to preserve the natural features of the parks, yet make them available for the pleasure of the people?

All parks are not alike. The very character and pur-

George B. Hartzog, Director, National Park Service.

pose of some parks limit their development and use. To attempt greater development and increased visitor use in some areas would destroy the very values for which the area is noted — and would deny to all visitors a certain unique experience which perhaps only that particular park could provide. Yellowstone National Park, for example, has a total gross area of about 2¼ million acres, yet less than five per cent of this area is occupied by physical facilities. The remainder of this great park has been set aside for the preservation of delicate and easily damaged phenomena and for the protection of the primitive wilderness with its plant and animal communities. Here, man is only a visitor and nature is supreme.

The Park Service, despite its name, is not a servant of the people in this direct and impossible sense — though we would be poor hosts indeed if we did not seek to make our visitors happy and pleased with their park experiences. Even though we are talking about public areas, I am convinced that it is not the responsibility of the administrators of such areas to comply with every use for which there is some public demand.

> —Because some segments of the public clamor for extensive road systems in parks and wilderness areas is not sufficient justification for uninhibited development. The consequence of yielding to these pressures would lead to a lower standard of quality in these natural areas.

—Because some people cannot walk and climb, or will not do so, does not justify building a road to every scenic overlook.

—Because some people want to ride motorcycles, mechanized carts and jeeps on foot paths and horse trails is no reason to allow them to do so on every trail.

—Because some people like to see wilderness from the veranda of a modern hotel is not sufficient justification for building hotels within national parks when their location outside a park would provide necessary accommodations without encroaching on the natural scene.

These facilities and enjoyments are entirely appropriate to certain areas. Tourism is wonderful, but the spirit of tourism should not, in my opinion, be the guiding principle of national park management.

Today, the accelerating rate of change in our society poses a major challenge to the National Park Service in its evolving management responsibilities. In response to this challenge, Director George Hartzog has developed a broad new program called *Parkscape U.S.A.* — based on three major objectives: growth in response to human need, cooperation with all concerned and innovation in ways to achieve the new conservation.

Director Hartzog's long range program includes five basic elements:

1. Completion of the National Park System Plan — including the identification of those remaining nationally significant natural, historical and recreational areas that may be suitably and feasibly included in the National Park System.

2. Through cooperative programs and joint planning with other organizations — Federal, state and local — seek creative new approaches for sharing know-how in park and recreation planning, development, maintenance, management, protection and interpretation.

3. Open the doors to exchanges of information and knowledge with other nations through an international park program.

4. Improvement and development of national parklands in and near urban areas where 75 per cent of the nation's population now resides.

5. Communicating to the American people, their magnificent heritage of natural, scientific and historical wonders.

During the past six years, the Congress has demonstrated a deep interest and concern with conservation matters through the enactment of such outstanding conservation legislation as the Land and Water Conservation Fund Act, the Wilderness Act, the Air Pollution Control Act, the Water Quality Control Act of 1965, the Highway Beautification Act, the Open Spaces Act, the Federal Water Projects Recreation Act, the Water Resources Planning Act, the Farm Act of 1965, creator of the Water Pollution Control Administration and its transfer to the Department of the Interior, and numerous others, all having some bearing on conservation, natural beauty and outdoor recreation.

In the last five years alone, some 33 areas — scenic, historic and recreational — have been added to America's growing system of national parklands, including our newest national park at Canyonlands in Utah.

We are reaching the end of the road in public domain suited to outdoor needs. Besides Canyonlands, perhaps we can establish a meaningful national park in the North Cascades in the State of Washington (see Appendix II) — and perhaps additional parklands in Alaska — out of land already owned by the public. But most of what we add to the national estate from now on, we will have to buy. We would hope that this would include a variety of types of recreation land — areas for high-density use and more remote lands as well — where we could partake of wilderness.

Fortunately, we have cracked the "not one cent for scenery" barrier by getting authorization to spend public money for the purchase of six magnificent seashores — Cape Cod, Padre Island, Point Reyes, Fire Island, Assateague Island and — most recently, Cape Lookout.

The National Park System was primarily and always will be in part, Western, because that is where the public lands still remain, and where we began to create a system. But with our new national seashores having been created, with the new national recreation areas, and some of the new park concepts that we have been developing, the Federal Government can and must do a major work in the East, before it is too late. In fact, we haven't quite talked about it that way, but most of the money, new money, that has been spent in recent years for acquisition has been spent either in the East or near the large cities. And I think this is overdue.

The Redwood Park proposal is an interesting variation of that. Among the nation's highest priorities for the protection of irreplaceable natural resources is the creation of a Redwood National Park in northern California. Here, are some of the world's most magnificent trees, including some virgin stands that will be logged over unless they are protected. Certainly these superb trees are a matter of significance and pride not only to Californians, but to all American people. I would like to see a large representative section of these incomparable forests preserved as a national park for all the people of this country.

Other major outdoor recreation proposals which President Johnson has recommended for approval are the Sleeping Bear and Indiana Dunes National Lakeshores bordering Lake Michigan, an Oregon Dunes National Seashore in Oregon, a Big Horn Canyon Na-

tional Recreation Area in Montana and Wyoming, a Great Basin National Park in Nevada, a Guadalupe National Park in Texas and Flaming Gorge National Recreation Area in Utah and Wyoming.

Three major eastern rivers — the Potomac, Hudson and Connecticut — are receiving, or should receive first priority attention in the cleansing of their waters, preserving the natural beauty of their stream banks and developing their recreational potential.

Also under active consideration are the proposed Apostle Islands National Lakeshore on Lake Superior in Wisconsin, and Voyageurs National Park in northern Minnesota. These would be complemented by the proposed Scenic Riverway which would preserve the wilderness qualities of the St. Croix and Namekagon Rivers in northern Wisconsin.

Accomplishment of these conservation objectives was brought one step closer for the American people with the passage of the Land and Water Conservation Fund Act of 1965. Now a major opportunity is provided to bring our supply of outdoor recreation areas and facilities closer to meeting our rapidly expanding demand. Charged with the administration of this fund is the Bureau of Outdoor Recreation. Forty per cent of the fund is available for Federal land acquisition by such agencies as the National Park Service, the U. S. Forest Service, the Bureau of Sport Fisheries and Wildlife and the U. S. Army Corps of Engineers, among others.

The remaining 60 per cent of the fund — presently an estimated $75 million or more a year — is to be available as matching grants to equal investments by states and local governments in the planning, acquisition and development of outdoor recreation areas and facilities.

In addition to the money, the grant program for the states also has produced several important corollary benefits. Most important has been the development of state-wide outdoor recreation plans — a prerequisite for eligibility for acquisition and development grants from the fund. Every state is now going through the process of determining a balanced outdoor recreation program to meet the needs of its people. By the end of 1966, most states should have completed the initial version of their outdoor recreation plan.

It is only fair to warn the American people that all of the recently authorized seashores, scenic riverways, and recreation areas will not be immediately available for public use. There *is* an important difference between "authorization" of an area which establishes its ultimate exterior boundaries, and the actual opening of the area to public use and enjoyment. If the lands are Federally owned — or if the land is state-owned and deeded over to the United States, as in the case of Cape Lookout — there is no problem. In most cases, however, these lands are in

13

private ownership and must be purchased.

In the face of rising land costs, we are leaning more and more toward such conservation innovations as "zoning" and "scenic easements," in lieu of outright purchase in fee. Even these relatively new instruments of resource protection have become more sophisticated in recent months as we now trend toward outright purchase of property and then "leaseback" or "sellback" to the original owners with appropriate easements and zoning provisions. Outstanding examples of this new approach are to be found at Point Reyes National Seashore, California; Ozark National Scenic Riverways in Missouri; and in the recent Merrywood case in the Washington, D. C., metropolitan area. Here, a jury recently awarded "just compensation" for the scenic easement taken by the Department of the Interior to prevent high-rise apartments from destroying the beauty of the Potomac River ~ge in the vicinity of the nation's capital.

~en with such innovations, there is yet another ~actor that we must consider in America's quest for new parks and recreation areas. The 40 per cent Federal share of the Land and Water Conservation Fund is simply not adequate presently to finance the timely acquisition of such areas. To purchase the lands required for the proposed Redwood National Park in California, for example, could entirely deplete the existing fund for this one project alone, and other land acquisition programs would have to be deferred. At the same time, there are certain irreplaceable areas that just cannot afford to wait, and which must be acquired in advance of the bulldozer and constantly spiraling land costs. Obviously, certain areas like the Coast Redwoods require a special appropriation.

For those who visit their parks frequently, the annual $7.00 gold-colored Federal Recreation Permit is a recreation bargain, valid from April 1 to March 31 of the following year. It serves as a vacation passport entitling the holder and all other occupants of his private, noncommercial vehicle to enter all Federal parks and recreation areas where an entrance fee is required. Money from the sale of the recreation permit goes into the Land and Water Conservation Fund — along with other Federal receipts — to provide additional Federal parks and recreation areas, and to assist the states in their outdoor recreation programs. Temporary and day-use permits are also for sale, but even if you never visit a national park, your purchase of the annual recreation permit will pay dividends by helping to insure to present and future generations a green legacy of parks, forests and other recreation areas.

Even with the advantages of the Land and Water Conservation Fund, it is going to take more than an en-

Mrs. Lyndon B. Johnson and Stewart L. Udall, Secretary of the Interior, at Grand Teton National Park.

larged public purse to acquire the much needed recreation and conservation areas, wildlife refuges, the scenic parks and city parks and playgrounds. A heightened sense of stewardship is a demanding challenge for those who are the private owners of open land — land which taken together, constitutes the largest conservation reservoir around our cities. Conservation of natural resources and the attainment of natural beauty are goals to which all citizens can contribute.

The answer to the mounting needs for expanding outdoor recreational opportunities does not lie wholly in an expanded National Park System. Part of the answer, at least, lies in improved management of areas already within the system.

Facilities in most parks — although vastly improved as a result of the ten-year *Mission 66* Program — are still inadequate to meet the stepped-up demands of the past decade. Over 121 million visitors entered areas of the National Park System in 1965, presenting the staff with the perennial problems on the one hand of providing for their accommodation, their recreation, their safety, their inspiration and enjoyment of park values — and, on the other hand, safeguarding the natural, historic and recreational resources which make up the very values they came to enjoy.

The continuing search for innovations that will make park visits more enjoyable has resulted in experimentation with such things as "one-way loop roads" that give the visitor a sense of being the first person on the scene.

With no traffic from the opposite direction, he can afford to take his eyes off the road and enjoy the historical and scenic attractions along the way. A fine example of this is the loop road through historic Cades Cove in the Great Smoky Mountains National Park.

Recreation by boat has created an increased need for construction of unobtrusive shoreline boat camps. The rapid increase in air travel for recreation purposes by private planes, and the desire for visitors to have air access to the parks have required the service to conduct a survey which determined requirements for airport or airstrip facilities in or in close proximity to the National Park System areas for this type of visitor.

More attention is being given to the encouragement of "winter camping" and other "off-season" vacation trips to spread out the traditional season of park use. This has already resulted in an extension of the season into spring, winter and fall without any decrease of visitor use in the peak months of June, July and August.

Man changes the natural environment in which he lives and upon which he depends, and makes increasing demands upon open space for his various needs. The dimensions of modifications and destruction may well alter the face of America beyond recall — with consequences to man's spiritual as well as material well-being. As the nation awakens to these multiplying problems of a multiplying population, the National Park Service has an important role to play in helping to reverse this trend.

The biotic associations within each park should be maintained — or where necessary, re-created — as nearly as possible in the condition that prevailed when the area was first visited by the white man. A national park should thus represent a vignette of primitive America. To assure that natural values are indeed preserved unimpaired for future generations, the National Park Service has recognized the need for a stepped-up research program in accordance with the recommendations of the Advisory Board on Wildlife Management. We are learning that protection alone is not enough.

Park environments are not stable entities. Plant communities as well as wildlife populations are subject to external influences — particularly the direct impact of human use — and fragile resources can be easily depleted or destroyed. Only in recent years have conservationists become vitally concerned with the fact that park boundaries drawn on a map are no proof against the modern world of power and irrigation projects, of pesticides and polluted water, of science working its miracles and of the increasing demands for outdoor recreation by an ever-multiplying population. Competition for space between visitors and certain forms of wildlife can result in conflict. Sound resource management programs based upon current knowledge and supplemented by research are essential to ensure that the long range objectives and goals of the National Park Service will be fulfilled.

Visitors to parks, forests, wilderness areas and the like can get enjoyment and benefit from untutored and unsophisticated experiences. Beauty can be appreciated without someone pointing and saying: "See. Isn't that beautiful?" But for many people, the capacity for pleasure from an outdoor experience can be greatly enhanced by understanding. One of the hallmarks of the National Park Service has always been its interpretive programs — "communicating a message." A person can come to the great scenic places preserved in our parks and be inspired, but for a lasting understanding of "what all this is about," he needs to have such knowledge communicated to him.

While the parks themselves are vast museums out-of-doors, alive and ever changing, the full dynamics of a region can seldom be seen outdoors. This requires a museum within walls. At visitor centers throughout the National Park System, visitors can study the geologic forces that have changed the land, the evolution of ecologies — the flora and fauna — the influence of man — ancient and modern — on the landscape. A few hours spent inside a museum, using the latest communications and interpretive techniques, provides the visitor with a better appreciation of things he sees outside.

Personally conducted interpretive programs — epitomized by the campfire programs and guided tours — are considered the most meaningful interpretive activities experienced by park visitors. Yet, the effectiveness of these services has been greatly reduced because of the escalating increase in travel to parks and insufficient manpower to conduct these popular activities.

In many parks, it has become necessary to rely heavily upon self-guiding and audio-visual devices to take up much of the interpretive load. Self-guiding facilities capable of handling greater numbers of people are being developed, and the use of self-guiding leaflets and free distribution material is increasing rapidly.

In this way it is becoming possible for the Park Service to communicate to more and more people the genuine values and pleasures of our national parks and other areas under its administration. From Acadia National Park in Maine to Sequoia in California, from Mount McKinley National Park in Alaska to Everglades in Florida, Americans should be better able to appreciate their truly remarkable natural heritage.

Washington, D. C.

ACADIA

LOCATION: Maine
(primarily Mount Desert Island)
SIZE: 32,197* acres
ESTABLISHED: 1919

There is an air of aristocracy about Acadia National Park, but nothing of the luke-warm, weak-tea flavor that sometimes surrounds that word. It is an "aristocrat" in the same sense that the noble Americans who first tried to preserve this place were called by that name — because they could appreciate the many moods of dashing splendor in man and nature.

Acadia National Park holds itself sometimes aloof in fog-shrouded mystery and sometimes spreads its inner resources of sea and sunshine with a lavish freedom born of ancient riches. Sometimes it flaunts its elegance unconcerned and unquestioning, and sometimes, with an overplus of hospitality, it opens its arms to any who come to its door.

It was here, after the Civil War, that the first families of America's inherited wealth came and invited the leisure classes of the world to join them for their summer pleasures. Like called to like, and those of princely tastes came to these islands of royal beauty.

Here is the pink granite of Cadillac Mountain (highest point on the Eastern Seaboard); here is the wild crashing sea surging into Thunder Hole; here are the wide, still waters of Somes Sound; here is the variety and grandeur of nature that brought the wealthy socialites of a by-gone age to vacation at Bar Harbor at the turn of this century.

This society has passed away. The Bar Harbor "cottager" whose "cottage" required a dozen household servants to maintain is no longer the chief visitor to Acadia, now, since 1919, a national park (called Lafayette National Park until 1929). The new aristocrat, the American vacationer appreciative of nature's wonders, comes bringing his family to this graceful leisure land where the smell of the great spruce forests and the briny tang of the sea, and the tangle of blueberries there for the picking, and the fish-filled streams for his rod and reel, and the lobster traps that are emptied at morning for his purchasing, these all let a man live like a king.

The name "Acadia" was first used in ancient Greece (in the form of "Arcadia") to mean a place of rest and delight-in-nature. Early French colonists found the name appropriate for the lands they settled in southeastern Canada, and when the area around Bar Harbor, Maine, became the first national park east of the Mississippi, it was appropriate that eventually it would be called Acadia National Park.

Most of the park is on Mount Desert Island which was discovered by Champlain in 1604. He named it "L'Isle de Monts-deserts," that is, "The Island of the Solitary Mountains." Jesuit missionaries settled there in the early 17th century to teach the Abnaki Indians who gathered there in the summer to harvest berries and to fish.

*This figure refers only to Federally controlled land and does not include state, county or private holdings within park boundaries. For gross acreages, see Appendix.

Plunging 107 feet into the Atlantic Ocean are the Otter Cliffs where the struggle between land and sea continues. Gulls and other birds dive for fish here and hoards of migrating sea ducks float by each season.

Other European settlers, French and English, followed. There were frequent clashes between these groups, but by 1759 France had relinquished its claim to the area, and New Englanders had established a settlement on Somes Sound (the only fjord on the New England Coast).

In 1820 Maine became a state and what is now Acadia National Park supported a thinly settled fishing economy. But during the 19th century artists rediscovered the beauty of the area, and summer boats from Boston brought it out of the wilderness and within the reach of the affluent, who responded to its loveliness. They came, summer after summer, building fashionable homes and fashioning an elegant summer society around themselves.

In 1901 some of those vacationers, fearful that the beauty of their island would be ravaged by commercial exploitation, formed a corporation "to acquire and hold for public use lands in Hancock County, Maine, [because of their] beauty [and] historical interest. . . ." They donated a square rod of land "for public use" [that is about 16 feet square: room enough perhaps for a bench and a drinking fountain), and in a dozen years had acquired about 6,000 additional acres. The corporation donated this land to the Federal Government, which, in 1916,

created out of this gift the 50 square miles that now make up Acadia National Park.

East of Mount Desert Island, across Frenchman Bay, there is another portion of the park on Schoodic Peninsula, and southwest of Mount Desert is the park's truly isolated wilderness of Isle au Haut ("High Island") which can be reached only by boat.

But to most of the visitors, who arrive in great numbers only to be swallowed by the winding trails and sheltered glens and surf-tossed beaches, Acadia National Park lies along the loop of Ocean Drive—a major park road curving along the Atlantic, gliding in and out of spruce and fir forests, dipping beside quiet inland ponds, suddenly surprising a feeding band of deer that with unfrightened speed gracefully vault into the deeper forest on one side of the road, with the elegance of the yachts, large and small, seen in the distance on the road's other side, sailboats spreading their chalk-white sails along the deep blue sea around them.

Most visitors come to Acadia in the summer, but spring and fall are pleasant too and the park is more one's own. Cool nights and rain are known to all three seasons. It is only winter — from December through April when snow and ice close the park road system — that is inhospitable.

*S*choodic Point (above) is at the tip of Schoodic Peninsula, the only part of Acadia National Park located on the mainland. There, a young boy (left) feeds near-tame sea gulls on the rocks. Acadia's rockbound coast (far left) has come from centuries of ocean wear. On these shorelines, children can find a myriad of treasures mixed in with the ocean-smoothed rock; enough sea shells for a collection.

The common egret (above left) was almost exterminated by plume hunters but now is Federally protected. Boaters (above right) still come to Bar Harbor. A sunset enhances Acadia's solitary feeling (below).

Acadia's miles of cliffs and rocky shorelines are easily accessible by scenic roads. Trails for hiking and for horses reach almost every spot in the park, varying from easy paths to rugged mountain routes.

BIG BEND

LOCATION: Southwestern Texas
SIZE: 706,538 acres
ESTABLISHED: 1944

The Great River, the Rio Grande, running a fairly straight southeast course, edging the United States and Mexico across the Chihuahua desert, suddenly bends around to its left, cuts to the north past the Chisos Mountains—for a total of 107 miles. And before it turns south again it puts a heart-shaped lower boundary on Big Bend National Park.

Here is the wilderness. Here is the unexplored. Here is the West (with a capital letter) in all of its desert and mountain and storybook wildness.

In this day of overcrowding bustle and hustle and nudging neighbors, parts of Big Bend National Park, which is within 300 miles of El Paso, Texas, and 400 miles of San Antonio, are still not fully explored. Parts of it are so untouched by this world of the 20th century that a vacationer can ride his horse out from the comforts of a modern resort area and within an hour feel that he is alone in a world, uninhabited, untouched, and perhaps—before he himself looked upon it—unseen.

This is a proud solitary stretch of country, harsh without bitterness, austere without anger and silent with a proud and brooding unfathomable mystery.

Even the suddenly green pockets of lush cotton-wood-lined oases along the river's edge seem like gentle guests (rather than settlers) of the sweeping mesa and rolling mountain land that tolerate their being there with the preoccupied hospitality of a host who has great matters on his mind.

This area has never been an easy one to know. It grudgingly permitted some acquaintanceship, but never sought or welcomed friendship; and it never offered itself or its resources to explorers or ranchers or miners or farmers. It wasn't until 1899 that anyone made a trip of record around the "big bend" of the Rio Grande. Others may have gone there before Robert T. Hill and five companions explored it for the Geological Survey in 1850, but the others went to raid, to smuggle or to hide.

Men who went there before the days of the park's development went there usually driven by motives which seemed better concealed than advertised. Train robbers, bank robbers, American fugitives, Mexican bandits slipped in and out of the area as they slipped in and out of the history of the outlaw-gunman West. Here, as late as 1916, Mexican bandits, possibly some of Pancho Villa's men, invaded the United States.

But today the men of violence are gone. Today if

The century plant stands before the Chisos Mountains in Green Gulch. The Chisos add a sense of adventure to their mysterious past: it was here that dinosaurs roamed before lava pushed upward to become mountains.

the visitor hears rustling in the underbrush, it is probably not a cattle rustler but a juvelina or a mule deer, or a cougar or a white tailed deer.

In the middle of the park, the Chisos Mountains rise up like a string of fortified castles set to hold back the advance of the hordes of sage and cactus on the desert floor. The mountains throw their forest troops into battle lines against the invaders. In the front rank are the stunted oak and drooping juniper, and on the higher ground, the piñon pine and Douglas fir and ponderosa pine.

The name of these mountains, "Chisos," is hard to translate. Part Indian, part Spanish, it carries the idea of ghostly wonder or enchantment in and out of both languages. And these mountains speak the mystery that surrounds Big Bend National Park.

Looking south from their south rim, a visitor knows in his mind that he is looking towards Mexico, but in the clear bright air and the isolated silence of a seemingly never-ending distance his heart begins to feel that he is looking over the edge of the world itself. He feels for just a moment on the edge of time itself so that, as a local saying has it, standing here on the side of the mountains of mystery, "on a clear day, you can see clear into the day after tomorrow."

Flowers begin to bloom in the lowlands in late February but do not reach the mountain heights until May. Spring also brings occasional "northers," sudden storms that bring chill winds and often dust. The mountains are particularly attractive in the summer when temperatures in the desert and valley hover around 100 degrees. With the end of autumn—warm, gentle and delicately colored—comes the sparkling clear air of winter. Once or twice a year snow comes to the mountains, but usually in winter the heights are merely brisk while the canyons remain comfortably warm during the day.

The river and mountains have given the park

three large canyons. Boquillas—or "Little Mouth"—is where the river cuts the Sierra del Carmen in two. In some places it cuts with the stroke of a butcher's cleaver that slices the rock straight down to the water's edge, and in other places it hacks with hatchet chops that send chips of sand and tangles of willow a few feet up the bank.

But up river in the Santa Elena Canyon the Rio cuts the walls of the Grand Puerta ("Great Door") with a 1,500-foot slash of its knife edge.

The third canyon, Mariscal ("Marshall"), is most remote, most difficult to reach, and most rewarding. Mariscal allows only boatmen to explore its limestone walls and view the fossilized remains of animals who lived in those distant ages of the deep past of our earth—times that still seem close beside the traveler within the remote and mystic silence and emptiness and untouched grandeur that is Big Bend National Park.

Santa Elena Canyon (above) continues for 17 miles while sheer rock walls form a box-like gorge around it. Here, the Rio Grande is an international border, with Mexico on the left. Further along the river is Boquillas, Mexico, (far left) an old village seated below the Sierra del Carmen. In the northern section of Big Bend is Dagger Flat, where the giant dagger yucca (left) is found. Big Bend is the only place in the United States where the giant dagger has grown.

Queen Victoria (above) stands in the Queen's Garden below Sunrise Point. Variations in the weather and erosion resistance of the rock layers account for the unusually interesting forms at Bryce Canyon. Systems of cracks and joints have created such phenomena as the Natural Bridge (right) which was cut from the famous Pink Cliffs. The varying intensities of red are the result of the iron content of the rock.

BRYCE
CANYON

LOCATION: Southern Utah
SIZE: 36,010 acres
ESTABLISHED: 1928

To enter Bryce Canyon is to come upon a unique world set in the middle of an already spectacular country. Its pinnacles and spires, in their strange, almost Gothic delicacy, create an impression that they are related to rock as lace is to fabric. The canyon is weird and other-worldly and at the same time inescapably an elemental, sculptural part of Earth. There *is* creation in destruction, and Utah's Bryce Canyon National Park is a silent, slowly evolving example of the forces of water seeking lower levels.

Stretching for about 30 miles along the eastern edge of 8,000-foot Paunsaugunt Plateau are the famous Pink Cliffs, one of the finest of Utah's eroded landscapes. Primordial forms (sometimes called "castles" and "temples"), have been constructed by the relentless forces of water rushing down the slopes of the plateau.

From atop the plateau rim, one looks out over the Bryce Amphitheatre and the Silent City, or into the narrows of the canyon called Wall Street, or over the vast expanse of land to the east and southeast where the Paria River for millenniums has capriciously cut, gouged and torn away layer upon layer of rock. The river and some relatively pencil-thin streams are now nibbling away at the rate of two feet every century.

The plateau is the edge of a bowl of color — oranges, reds, whites, pinks, yellows and purples interspersed with gentle browns, reflecting the changing light, from sunrise to sunset, from storm to sunshine, from summer to winter. Hardy visitors get a different and exciting glimpse of one of the superlatives of nature's handiwork, while hiking below the rim among the eerie but beautiful erosion remnants of the Wasatch-limestone formations.

Bryce Canyon's history began long before the Paiute Indians gave Paunsautgunt ("home of the beaver") Plateau its name and called the area, "red rocks standing like men in a bowl-shaped canyon." It was 60 million years ago that inland lakes and seas started to lay down on this area deposits of silt, sand and lime in beds as much as 2,000-feet thick. The deposition of the Bryce strata ended about 25 million years ago and the lands of southern Utah began to rise slowly. During this gradual elevation, produced by pressure within the earth, beds of rock were broken into blocks many miles in width and length. Some blocks were raised more than others, producing seven plateaus.

One of the area's early settlers was Ebenezer Bryce for whom the park is named. He pastured cattle here in the late 1870's and made the famous remark that it was "a hell of a place to find a stray cow." But it wasn't until the early 20th century that the remote canyon began to gain recognition as a potential park.

Today the park is everywhere enhanced by the trees, shrubs and flowers that nature has so expertly placed. Stately ponderosa pines, very old weather-beaten bristlecone pines, spruce, fir and junipers all abound. These in turn give a setting for the colorful birds, deer, fox and many other forms of wildlife. Bryce is geologically the youngest of the trio of truly great Southwest canyons, as unique in its own way as its older brothers, Grand and Zion.

A vivid contrast to the Pink Cliffs (above) is the three-foot snow that covers the area several months each year. Standing rigidly above the spires of Campbell Canyon is Boat Mesa (right) which rises over 8,000 feet.

CANYONLANDS

LOCATION: Southeastern Utah
SIZE: 257,640 acres
ESTABLISHED: 1964

No one will visit Canyonlands, the newest of our national parks, in southeastern Utah for some time to come without making very special preparations. Although there are park rangers stationed in each district of the park, even the rangers have their headquarters at the town of Moab, outside the park itself, and the tourist accustomed to roughing it in campsites where fuel can be bought and water is available will find even these primitive conveniences missing at Canyonlands.

Presently, and for perhaps the next few years, the tourist in Canyonlands will have to be a self-sufficient camper, and above that he will have to be something of a pioneer and an explorer too. He will find the summer days are very hot and the summer nights are mild. The roads, he will also find, are, at their best, rough and narrow, but the dramatic scenery, and the sense of being alone in the sweeping wonder of nature in the land of nature's last secret seclusion, will be reward enough for those who are prepared to accept it.

The center of Canyonlands is where the Green and the Colorado Rivers come together. And all around the confluence of these streams, the land is laced with tangles of small gorges down which, after a sudden cloudburst, a raging torrent will smash its violent way for an hour and then leave a dry and soon-dusty creek bed for perhaps another year, or even longer. Since the beginning of time this cut and slash of water has eaten away the land into a complex mass of sand and sagebrush and sandstone that is unmatched for variety. The heavier and constant flow of the main rivers, the Green and the Colorado, have scooped out three large intersecting areas, between which it is difficult to move.

Some people have been lucky enough to sight-see Canyonlands from a helicopter. Light, low-flying airplanes have given others a sweeping panoramic glance at all of its treasures. With daring, experienced skill, and special boats it is possible to run through the now lazy, now rasping, tumbling, terrible waters of Cataract Canyon. Other waters can be traveled by rubber rafts, pontoons or motor boats. But for most of the park's modern vacation-explorers transportation is a tough, well-sprung car. And then there are some places one can only reach by walking, and yet still others to which you have to climb.

There are three entries to the park. Coming in from the north, between the rivers, the visitor moves along the skyline plateau to Grandview Point, on the southern tip of Island in the Sky, from which a great sweep of the park's high desert wilderness may be seen. Looking back to the north and west one can see the red round lift of Upheaval Dome which seems to bubble out of the earth's crust; and looking forward below him, the esplanade of White Rim, in a southern semicircle, puts a catwalk around the inner gorges. From there one looks down into smaller arroyos, embayments and basins of lesser canyons.

West of the meeting of the rivers is the Land of Standing Rocks and a network of little-known, interlocking gullies and buttes called The Maze, which are not presently within the park's boundaries. Most of this area is broad upland plateau made up of vast, wild, overlaying, twisted and broken layers of rock — worn away by wind and occasional rain into shapes

The view south from Grandview Point shows variety in the canyons from mesas to spires, cliffs to plateaus.

that would seem to be the work of a madman.

The southeast section of the park, known as The Needles, is perhaps its most exciting part. Here the sandstone has been broken and eroded and pushed about into a jumble of pillars thrust-up, arches thrown-out and valley stamped-down into shapes so unusual that the visitor must learn new words to describe them.

The Grabens (from the German word for "ditch") are places where the land seems to have dropped down an elevator shaft, leaving behind them immense flat-bottomed valleys of stone bordered by vertical walls. And as the visitor comes upon these Grabens in this section of the park, such is the immensity of the surrounding distance, that what are deep faults in the earth's crust seem much smaller than they are.

Famous Druid Arch is also in this southeastern section of the park. Squarer than other natural-span formations, this arch looks like three balanced druid stones taken from England's mysterious Stonehenge on the Salisbury Plain — except that these rocks have

been multimagnified many times: instead of the menhirs being twice as high as a man can reach, these are about 220 feet high.

In this part of Canyonlands long departed Indians, or their predecessors, have left their mark. Storehouses of grain, with the corn still in them and dried iron-hard by a thousand summers, are still standing almost as they were left. Palm prints of prehistoric man are still visible on the walls of some caves. And at Newspaper Rock (outside Canyonlands' boundaries, at Utah's Indian Creek State Park, on the approach road to The Needles) the visitor can read the pictographs that someone scratched there on the "desert varnish" of the cliff. Here are man and animals, houses and hunters, circles and snakes, and symbolic rivers that must have meant something once to those who could read what was written here. But now these simple scratches on the canyon wall add to the wonderful solitude of Canyonlands' great empty space, another mysterious dimension of silence in the dim, forgotten past.

*A*lthough Angel Arch (far left) has an opening 190 feet high, one sees its true size only by noticing the three men who are waving their hats from the inside right of the base. Druid Arch (left), like Angel Arch, is in The Needles area which provides the true scenery of erosion. Sandstone, broken into blocks by close-set joints, was eroded to form pillars, spires and balanced rocks. Strangely, the sandstone nearby was eroded into sunken valleys and swirls (below).

In some cases, the approaches to a national park are as interesting as the park itself. Canyonlands, which at this date is accessible to only the hardy, is one of these parks. At Deadhorse Point (below), just north of the park, is a mighty view of the Colorado River winding into Canyonlands. From the same location (right), the varied, rugged nature of Canyonlands is apparent. A jeep road makes its way between the cliffs only through the efforts of husky, energetic men (below right) who have developed it.

CARLSBAD CAVERNS

LOCATION: Southeastern New Mexico
SIZE: 46,113 acres
ESTABLISHED: 1930

Plunging to a known depth of 1,100 feet are the Carlsbad Caverns, hollowed by seeping groundwater in limestone beds laid down by an ancient sea. Appropriately named, the Big Room (above) has 14 acres of floor space; at one point the ceiling arches 285 feet above the mile-long perimeter trail. Formations (left) include stalactites on the ceiling, stalagmites on the floor, columns and twisting helictites.

If one person can be credited with initially exploring the yawning depths of Carlsbad Caverns, in the contemporary record of man, it is a determined, brave and dedicated cowboy named James Larkin White, who descended into these incredible hollows in 1901.

Prior to his descent, this now world-famous national park of southeastern New Mexico had been known to a handful of ranchers, when the austere desert lands of the Guadalupe Mountains were settled just after the Civil War. But like most of our great natural wonders, the existence of the caverns was known to the Indians of the region and their forebears for many centuries prior to the incursions of the white man.

Cooking pits, colored clay paintings or pictographs attest to historic and prehistoric habitation in the sheltering vaulted arch of the caverns entrance.

For many years the awesome depths were known simply as the Bat Cave, from which hordes of the insect-eating mammals came wheeling and fluttering each summer day at sunset.

White so graphically described the bizarre features of this underground wonderland that the official interest of the General Land Office was aroused in 1923, and Robert A. Holley was assigned to investigate the authenticity of this vast natural wonder as an area possibly worthy of national preservation.

After 30 days of exploration, Holley was moved to state: "I am wholly conscious of the feebleness of my efforts to convey in words the deep, conflicting emotions, the feelings of fear and awe, and the desire for an inspired understanding of the Divine Creator's work which presents to the human eye such a complex aggregate of natural wonders in such a limited space."

On the basis of Robert Holley's enthusiastic official report, bolstered by the indefatigable efforts of James Larkin White, Carlsbad Cave was established as a national monument in 1923 and reestablished as a national park in 1930. Since then, about 13 million visitors have experienced the profound awe of both White and Holley. The breathtaking height of ceiling, the vastness of many-acred floor areas, the variety of exquisite forms to be seen on cavern roofs, walls and floors present proof that this is one of our na-

tion's most interesting and popular preservations.

On the surface of the park, especially in spring, there is a variety of colorful and bustling desert life. Birds, reptiles, raccoons, lizards and vultures thrive in the mountain-desert aridity which is emblazoned with the bright yellows of the bladderpod and prickly pear blossoms and blended with purple verbena and whitish pepperweed. Daytime temperatures in summer can be high, but evenings are cool. As summer wanes, the hillsides lose their color and reptiles go into hibernation beneath rocks. In winter the temperatures are mild, snow and ice are rare. Juncos, towhee and pyrrhuloxias become the most conspicuous of the birds.

And the bats still arrive en masse in spring, their return heralding the nightly tumbling black clouds of foraging flight emerging from the maw of the caverns. There is a proliferation of young bats each summer, but the chill frosts of November kill the insect provender, and mass migration southward again throws up a weird and sinuous cloud against exotic desert horizons.

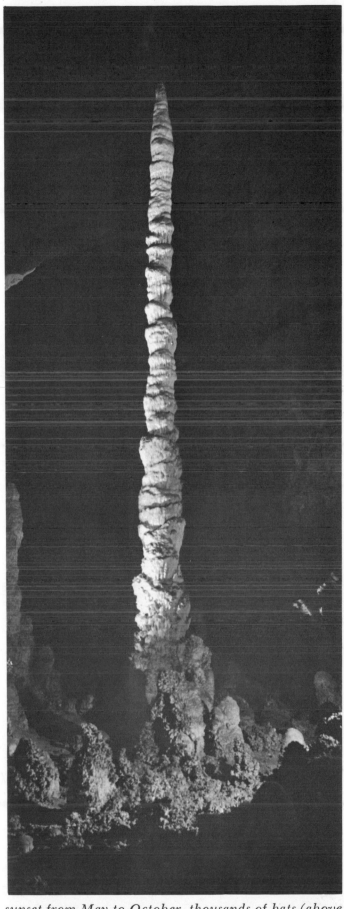

Temple of the Sun (opposite) stands in the Big Room. At sunset from May to October, thousands of bats (above left) spiral from the entrance in search of food. Totem Pole (above right) is a huge, 40-foot stalagmite.

Wizard Island (above), situated in Crater Lake, is actually a volcano within a volcano. The caldera holding Crater Lake was formed when the volcanic cone of Mount Mazama collapsed. Visitors can take boat trips on this deep blue lake and even climb into the 90-foot-deep crater of Wizard Island. A 35-mile drive around the rim shows the size and scenic grandeur of the lake. Heavy snows from the moisture-filled clouds from the Pacific Ocean result in 50 feet of snow annually which lace the trees and shrubs (right) and delight photographers. Despite such heavy snowfalls, the park stays open all year.

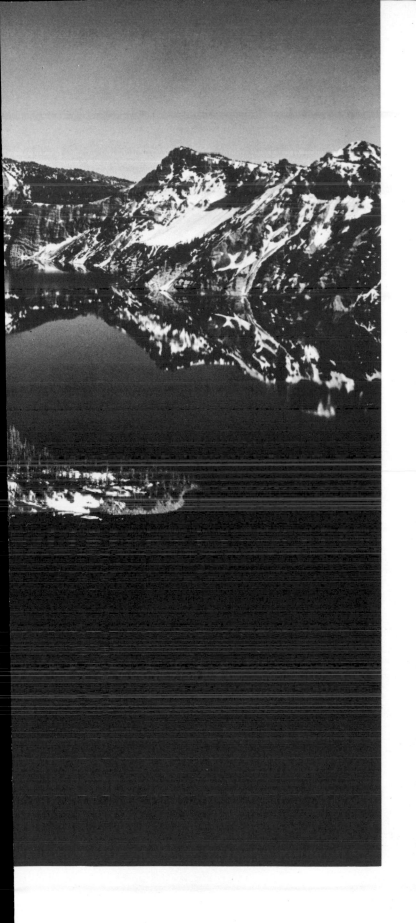

CRATER LAKE

LOCATION: Southwest-Central Oregon
SIZE: 160,290 acres
ESTABLISHED: 1902

A quarrel between two mighty Indian gods created Oregon's Crater Lake—so goes the lore of the local prehistoric Indians who tell us that the earth collapsed to a depth of almost 2,000 feet, forming the circular lake's basin, because of a raging struggle between "chief of the world above" and "chief of the world below."

The myth, not quite as old as the actual geological earth movement of 7,000 years ago, which carved out the second deepest lake in the Western Hemisphere, tells us that the underworld deity retreated below just as the chief of the upper regions let fall a mountain top on any possible exit to the surface.

Yet science more factually hypothesizes that predecessors of the Indian myth-makers may have seen the collapse of volcanic Mount Mazama, thousands of years ago, and built their myth, like most myths, on a residue of fact.

Crater Lake, astride the Cascade Range, thence gathered to itself the snows and rains of centuries, tinged gradually into the vast and stunning royal blue of its present setting.

It is said that the lake has only two seasons: an eight-month, snow-shrouded winter and an Eden-like two-month summer. But there is a brief snow-melting spring, and a haunting, chill-touched momentary fall. Yet, in all seasons, there endures the onslaught of arboreal beauty with hemlock, fir and pine clothing the pumiced slopes in varied shades of green, dappling the warm tones of summer and richly dotting winter's wide, white mantle.

Mount Scott, highest point in the park at 8,926 feet,

commands the eastern side of the lake and overlooks blue waters 20 square miles in area. Multicolored canyon-like walls, 500 to 2,000 feet high, surround the crater depths of water, their heights majestic with conifers and bleak with sporadic barren surfaces.

The Pinnacles, near the eastern boundary, also contribute to the mute but striking evidence of earth forces that here wrought violence in the Olympian shaping of the now serene landscape.

John Wesley Hillman recalled, many years later, his initial encounter with Crater Lake on June 12, 1853. Only 21, he was perhaps the first white man to look upon Deep Blue Lake, as his party of exploration chose to call it. His recollection: "It is really an impossibility to describe this lake as I first viewed it. The vast loneliness of the place, the sparkling water so many feet below, the beautiful view of the whole thing are all too great to be described; one must see them to appreciate them."

Others followed Hillman, but not until 1869 did visitors from Jacksonville give the vast volcanic repository of handsome waters its present name.

William Gladstone Steel is outstanding among the lake's subsequent admirers. He came, for the first of many visits, to the brink on August 15, 1885. A six-day sojourn lengthened into a lifetime rendezvous. On one trip, in 1888, Steel was inspired to comment: "Standing alone, like a sentinel on the mountains of the Far West, [Crater Lake] looks down on the sleeping grandeur about it and is unique in all the world. The day is coming when the people of all nations will gather to view its grandeur, then return to their homes to wonder that such things can be."

This indeed was a prophecy, aided and abetted by his own dedication and labors. Leader of the 17-year campaign to create a national park, he achieved this goal when, on May 22, 1902, President Theodore Roosevelt signed the bill conferring on the wondrous waters their present status. Will Steel, later superintendent and U.S. commissioner for the park, has since been informally and gratefully called: "Father of Crater Lake National Park."

Thus was the immortal blue of Crater Lake preserved for the beneficence of mortal man and his posterity.

A golden-mantled ground squirrel, often confused with a chipmunk, is very popular with park visitors.

The Phantom Ship (opposite), with 175-foot spires, "floats" before the lava cliffs that surround the second deepest lake in this hemisphere. The 8,926-foot Mount Scott (above) is the highest point at Crater Lake.

EVERGLADES

LOCATION: Southern Florida
SIZE: 1,306,509 acres
ESTABLISHED: 1947

Known for its birdlife and open spaces, Everglades was called "Pa-hay-okee" or "grassy waters" (above) by the Indians. The osprey (left), the only hawk that dives into water, sails toward his nest in a dead tree.

Quiet, calm, flat, mysterious — the Everglades are a unique part of the American landscape, the largest subtropical wilderness in North America.

The Calusa and Tequesta Indians first settled here, flourishing among the mangroves and thriving on the rich fish and game varieties in swamp and stream. Both groups dwelt in this sweeping, water-haunted lushness before the beginning of the Christian era. The Calusa, however, survived as an identifiable tribe for 250 years after the Spanish explorers arrived in the 16th century.

The legend of the fierce, quaintly bonneted, and riotously painted Seminole Indians, whom we more familiarly associate with the Everglades, goes back to the early 19th century when that tribe fled the plains before the U.S. Cavalry. Now, they fish in the park, amid nostalgic overtones.

Lake Okeechobee, massively spilling over to the north, created this river of grass, broad, short and shallow, with multifarious water creatures thriving in and about its swampy lushness, characterizing the biological wealth of the area.

Leggy, wading birds lift their fishy meals from the waters; alligators, turtles, otter and fish flutter, creep and splash in natural patterns through the willows, submerged roots, drenched grass and spatterdock.

All this lush, growing green can be seen best from the jungle spots on elevated islands which are called hammocks. Towering trees, dangling vines, carpets of ferns, West Indian in character, flourish here, where thrive the Liguus tree snails, so beautiful in aspect and so rarely seen elsewhere.

Here, where dark, tangled coastal forests drove Spanish horsemen to more maneuverable coasts, are ghostly clusters of mangrove trees, cypress heads, bay-heads and stands of Caribbean pine. Many trees grow above tangles of crooked roots which sustain their trunks above the water. The roots interlock and are a hazard to the legs of men landing from pole-propelled flatboats. The pines are slender-tufted, fire-resistant and fire-perpetuated and they have been used extensively in the building of termite and rot-resistant structures.

Hauntingly characteristic of the demesne is the whispering in the pinelands aroused by the slightest breeze, wafting a heady fragrance through the trails frequented by students of nature.

These tree concentrations are called "the mountains of the glades" rising with their own minute majesty only seven feet above sea level. Yet even in the wettest seasons they are not inundated. This is the plashy purlieu of the raccoon, the bobcat, quail and turkey.

The Everglades thermometers do not fluctuate sharply during the two characteristic seasons, the wet summer and dry winter. But the two contrasting seasons obviously influence the wildlife, with bird and beast migrating in winter to surviving water areas in great numbers.

During the rainy season, great cloud formations are sculptured battlements over the terrain, colored and dominated by dark thunderheads. The clouds progressively reach an explosive peak, then burst with a great rush, pouring down the life-giving rain. Some-

45

times a hurricane will move in from the tropical seas, wreaking havoc on trees, branches, birds and fish in mighty climax over the park. Sea beasts are washed ashore in the wake of the storm's anger; vegetation stands bare and wind-stripped; water everywhere, salt and fresh alike, inundates the land.

Midway to Flamingo from park headquarters, the salt area begins. This enormous brackish zone is nature's inaccessible nursery for numerous game fish and the coveted pink shrimp. Nature has providently arranged here a no-man's-land where predatory man and beast do not venture. Thus, spawn and prawn, a swampy matrix of infant, edible fish life, is permitted to grow and eventually fills the demands of

commercial and sport fish operations amid the Keys and along the Gulf Coast. This rich nursery of marine edibility actually is the basis of the well-known shrimp industry in the Tortugas.

Here, too, are the ghostly forests of mangrove trees, grotesque on the aforesaid prop roots, arching over sinuous waterways in hardy challenge to the boatman. The citizen of Copenhagen would wonder at the rookeries of storks in this region, increasing and multiplying, a continent removed from the storied stork-nest roofs of Denmark.

The dark memory of the ruthless plume hunters can be vividly recalled in this expanse, where ruthless exploiters once threatened to bring exquisite species

On Cape Sable the mangrove tree, which inhabits tidal marshes, stands on a maze of remarkable aerial roots.

of waterfowl to the point of extinction.

Flamingo, once a rustic, fishing village is now a gala gateway to the water wilderness of the park, the bays and rivers. Along the rich and intriguing Florida Bay shore there is no perceptible dividing line between land and sea. Beyond is Cape Sable, an arching shell beach, a pristine retreat whose immaculately white sands shelter the eggs of huge, lumbering loggerhead turtles, which may grow to weigh nearly half a ton.

The park by night is a jungle of sound and movement. The cries of night birds, the watery thrashings of alligators seeking garfish in the sloughs, the crackling predatory movements of raccoons and panthers, the choruses of insects, toads and frogs arise in sporadic crescendo, and all are weirdly, momentarily illuminated by streaks of lightning in the ebony sky.

The experienced explorer knows the threat and rudeness of the terrain. The danger in some places of poisonous snakes (including the deadly diamondback rattlesnake), and trees which shake off blister-yielding rain drippings, the pits and pinnacles of the trails, make some tourists wary. Add to this the steamy humidity of summer, the severe winds and drenching rains. But the prize is worth the worry and strain. It now is attainable in areas of minimal discomfort for the bird-watcher, the naturalist, the boater. The strange beauty of the Everglades is ours.

One of the Everglades famous wading birds, the American egret spends the dry season (winter) in its rookery.

His head rising just above the water, a bull alligator (opposite, upper left) inflates his throat for a mating call. Differing from a crocodile in jaw and teeth formation, the alligator's biggest enemy, after maturity, is man. A frog (opposite, upper right) makes an interesting pattern while sunning itself on a palm leaf. The cougar or puma (opposite, below) sloshes along a tidal channel. It is seldom seen for there are only 100-300 left on the entire eastern seaboard, all in Florida. Everglades National Park is a good refuge for wildlife because hunting is prohibited. A small road off Florida State Highway 29 passes tall stately royal palm trees (above) which are native to southern Florida.

Two Seminole children (above) stand before their huts deep in the swamps near U.S. Highway 41. After Gen. Andrew Jackson ended the Seminole War (1817-1818), most Seminoles fled west, but many escaped to live in the glades of southern Florida. Their houses are built above ground, for low spots fill during the rainy season of summer. The wood and leaves from the palm tree (right) are used for Seminole homes.

Dead and rotting logs lay across a vast swamp (below) which is interlaced with placid waterways. At Everglades many tropical plants, as well as animals, are interspersed with plants and animals found in the temperate zone. This subtropical wilderness is the largest in North America. The cormorant (right), frequently seen in the Royal Palm Area, is an expert fisherman who often swims with just its neck and head showing and then dives sharply to pursue and capture a fish in its strongly hooked beak.

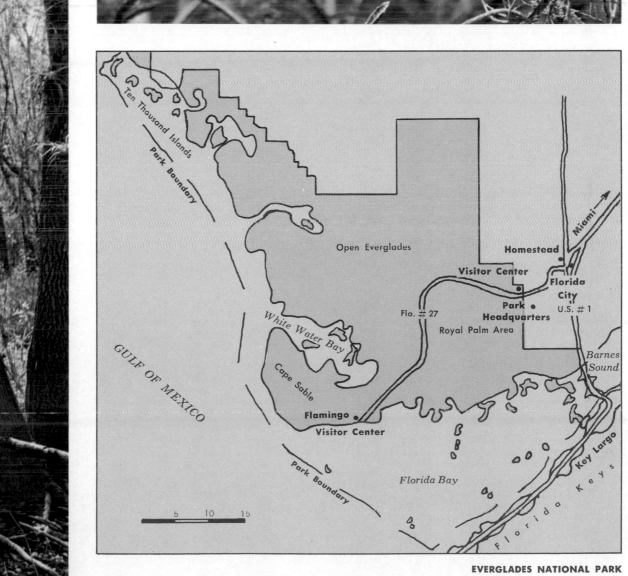

EVERGLADES NATIONAL PARK

Ten Thousand Islands

Park Boundary

Open Everglades

GULF OF MEXICO

White Water Bay

Cape Sable

Flamingo
Visitor Center

Park Boundary

Florida Bay

Fla. # 27

Royal Palm Area

Homestead

Visitor Center

Florida
City

Park
Headquarters

U.S. # 1

Miami

Barnes
Sound

Key Largo

Florida Keys

5   10   15

GLACIER

LOCATION: Northwestern Montana
SIZE: 1,010,308 acres
ESTABLISHED: 1910

Under the brooding storm clouds a sunrise reflects on Little Chief Mountain to the left and Citadel Mountain in the rear on the shore of St. Mary Lake. In 1932, Canada and the United States expressed good will by combining adjacent Glacier National Park in the United States and Waterton Lakes National Park in Canada into Glacier-Waterton International Peace Park.

Upper St. Mary Lake is an icy, elongated sphere of blue — a sapphire of water worn like a jewel, mirroring wisps of cotton clouds and wearing the sharp lines of surrounding mountains as the hands upon the face of a clock. The massive peaks, sheer, sharp walls of stone, are the rulers of this empire of trees and water and wildlife, flower-strewn meadows and living glaciers existing almost side by side in paradoxical enjoyment of their environments.

Here there are the seekers of this extraordinary beauty, the "Crown of the Continent," which includes more than a thousand miles of trails which lace through nearly 1,600 square miles of wild loveliness.

The ice-fingers of earth-evolution are not far from the velvety grass spread of hills and valleys sprinkled with summer flowers, one of the four biological life zones found here. Above are the spruce and fir, and surmounting them are subalpine plants, while still farther lie the colors — green, white and pastels — which hint at life in the most improbable places. Snow-capped peaks touch the limits of the sky a mile or more above the looking glasses of over 200 lakes.

The joyous sound of rushing water fills the spectator's ears, the pounding of diamond-blue streams cascading over moss-strewn stones and the never-ending roar of waterfalls tossing dancing crystals into the air above, defying time to stop their existence.

The geological history of the land is the foundation upon which this extraordinary beauty rests; plants and animals, fish and fowl are here because of the chain of events which evolved to form this panorama, from its rugged peaks mantled with snow to the green spread of meadows and valleys.

The heights arrived when the Rockies came into being 60 million years ago, but while that great stretch of peaks rose, new forces vised this Canadian-border region, bringing it sharply together, forcing the infant mountains sideways until finally the folded earth broke under the strain. The pressure continued, edging the land to the east for almost 40 miles.

Sedimentary layers — silts, sands, clays and muds — started it all a billion or two years ago in the shallow arm of a prehistoric sea. Chemical changes coupled with time and pressure solidified the layers, and they submerged, then emerged.

A million years ago, the valley floors lay beneath great glaciers which relentlessly ground downhill. They gave way years ago to smaller masses of ice, but not before the park's valleys were filled with ice three-fifths of a mile high. Then the earth became warm again, and magically the ice disappeared, then returned in lesser fury to cover the earth once more.

There is still preponderous evidence of the glaciers here, despite the warming trend. Nearly 300 acres are still covered by Sperry Glacier, about 400 feet deep, a latter-day, and comparatively miniscule, sample of what helped shape this region. Those flowing rivers of ice of a million years ago grabbed particles of sand and massive boulders, edging them along to rasp at the landscape and form today's rugged spectacle.

The hewn earth is a natural habitat for 57 species of animals and 210 bird species, some of which rest a day or two twice a year during migration.

The Rocky Mountain goat uses its soft-centered, splayed hooves to grasp the precarious cliffs, along with the pika and marmot and an occasional wolverine. In the deep, green depths of the forests live moose, elk, whitetail and mule deer, and black and grizzly bears. Above them wheel hawks and eagles, their telescopic eyes seeking food, and grouse escape in a thunder of wings from underfoot. Thrushes sing anonymously from the thick undergrowth, while the slaty-gray dipper flits along swiftly flowing streams. Harmonizing with the cacophony of bird sounds is the angry shriek of the jays preaching from the pulpit of treetops over the steady tree-drumming of the scarlet-crested pileated woodpecker, pausing only to vent its feelings about insect-hunting expeditions deep beneath tree bark. Beneath the surface of rushing streams and the translucent mirror of lakes live 22 species of fish: trout, salmon, whitefish, grayling.

It is little wonder Indians found their way here and chose it as a place to live for about 10,000 years. The Kutenai were displaced by the Blackfeet more than 200 years ago, and it was possibly their hostility that kept the Lewis and Clark expedition from the region. The Blackfeet received $1.5 million for their lands in 1890 when a copper strike was announced, and thus the region became open to a new generation of explorers.

Their reservation, an attraction in itself, adjoins

In early summer, yellow glacier lilies dot Logan Pass with color below the Garden Wall, seen to the north.

the park to the east where some of them sometimes gather in the colorful garb and feathered headdresses of their ancestors.

But color is not confined to the dyed feathers, for here is an area south of the Canadian border where a subarctic climate exists, giving life in short but magnificent splendor to alpine flowers. Up and down the great expanses of land are glacier lilies, their yellow blossoms contrasting with the blue of gentians and the scarlet of monkey-flowers. The lower landscapes are dominated by the cone-bearing trees, sometimes dripping needles upon Lake McDonald, the largest of the bodies of water, nestled in the loving grasp of western red cedar, with its fernlike leaves, hemlock and yew. The most common tree in the park is the lodgepole pine, which occurs on both slopes of the park, growing in pure stands or mixed with spruce, fir and Douglas fir. The needle-losing "evergreen" is the western larch. In autumn, its golden-yellow needles stand out in bright contrast against a background of forest greenery.

During the brief summer, sudden rain squalls or thundershowers may occur, and the higher elevations are cool at all times of the year. Even at the lower levels it is chilly after the sun sets.

The hasty traveler will see a part of this by driving across the park on the Going-to-the-Sun Road, the only road to cross the park. But this is only a hint of what lies beyond the long stretch of modern creation. A mountain never truly unfolds until one has stood at its feet or feasted upon the valleys below its peak; a green forest does not reveal its unique charms unless one stands under its pyramid spires; nor do nature's charms become fully apparent until one takes a few moments for silent appreciation. Glacier was meant to be felt, not idly viewed.

*B*eargrass (left), which is not a grass but a lily, blooms along the slope of 9,604-foot Going-to-the-Sun Mountain above Logan Pass Road. So common and showy is the beargrass that it is considered to be the park flower. With over 1,000 miles of trails, such as Skyline Trail (above), Glacier has the most extensive trail system of all the national parks.

Flowering until July, the Indian paintbrush (above left) decorates the Going-to-the-Sun Road. A close-up of the glacier lily (above right) which will grow on the edge of snow banks and sometimes up through the snow.

Flinsch Peak (opposite) is an excellent example of a cirque or amphitheatre caused by ice erosion. The potholes are also from glaciation. Pink monkey-flowers (below) bloom below the Garden Wall, a long cliff face.

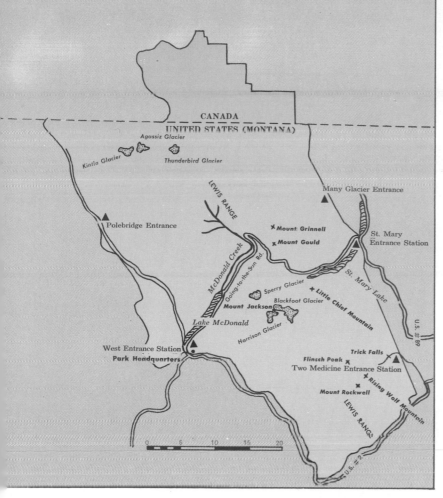

GLACIER NATIONAL PARK

*O*verlooking Two Medicine Valley (opposite, above) from abandoned lookout above Blackfeet Highway, one sees Rockwell Mountain in the center and Rising Wolf Mountain on the right. Light clouds cover 8,848-foot Mount Grinnell and Grinnell Glacier (opposite, below) on the eastern edge of the Continental Divide. The Trick Falls (left), in the Two Medicine area, is named because, in summer, after the melted snows of spring have subsided, the relatively low water flow is through a hidden opening in the base.

GRAND CANYON

LOCATION: Northwestern Arizona
SIZE: 673,203 acres
ESTABLISHED: 1919

At the Grand Canyon's South Rim, one stands at the brink of grandeur, looking over the Colorado to the higher North Rim. After Theodore Roosevelt's visit in 1903, he described the canyon "as the one great sight every American should see."

Late sunlight illuminates the walls of Deva, Brahma and Zoroaster "temples" near the North Rim.

Of all the geographic features of the United States that are famed for their scenic grandeur, the most extraordinary, the most truly unique, is the mile-deep canyon which the Colorado River has carved across the high plateaus of northwestern Arizona. . . . Though there are elsewhere deep canyons, some of even greater depth than the Grand Canyon, . . . there is not one that can match its vastness, its majesty, its ornate sculpture and its wealth of color. Whoever stands upon the brink of the Grand Canyon beholds a spectacle unrivaled on this earth.

FRANCOIS E. MATTHES, *The Grand Canyon of the Colorado River*

The wind blows gently down this vast wound in the earth, rippling the surface of its creative force, the river, and carrying occasional small puffs of red dust from the awesome walls. The breeze wanes and the eerie silence fans out in four directions, held captive within the impenetrable fortress nature spent nine million years to create.

The Grand Canyon is true to its name, yet a mere, momentary glance prods the beholder's mind, searching for a word more expressive than "Grand." The majestic, water-wrought stone sculpture is 217 miles long, averages a mile deep and spreads nine miles across in a panorama of pastels, each a page in the book of the canyon's continuing evolution.

In places where the bottom can be reached, the long hike or ride on muleback gradually unfolds in a geological layer cake — gray limestone walls formed when a long-forgotten sea shimmered in the prehistoric sunlight; green shale holding primitive fossils; pastel layer upon pastel layer, until finally millions of years have been passed in a drop of three-fifths of a mile. In the Inner Gorge are sheer walls growing progressively darker as they plunge toward the rushing Colorado River, walls so ancient they were formed before life on the earth, their fossilless bulk existing in the dark centuries when creation was building its foundation.

The river is still building the Grand Canyon, widening it and deepening it an unmeasurable, infinitesimal fraction of an inch each year. Where a narrow suspension bridge hangs frailly across the Colorado, the pulsating red torrent which carried, until the closure of Glen Canyon Dam in 1963, a half-million tons of soil downstream each day, each abrasive bit gently, imperceptibly wearing away at the captive walls, loosening other particles in the interminable process of erosion. Today it carries approximately one-sixth as much sediment.

In 1869 its vastness lured John Wesley Powell, the great explorer, here to lead a long and daring expedition through the treacherous canyons and gorges. The Spanish conquistadores stood upon its edge in the mid-1500's, and American trappers visited it in the 18th century, but it remained for Powell to conquer the Colorado.

A topographer, Lt. Joseph Christmas Ives, viewed the canyon in 1858, and later wrote, "It seems intended by nature that the Colorado River, along the greater portion of its lonely and majestic way, shall be forever unvisited and undisturbed." A geologist with Ives, John S. Newberry, did not share Ives' gloomy thoughts, and later interested Powell in the expedition. To Powell, the dangerous trip was a labor of unbridled joy. "Past these towering monuments, past these mounded billows of orange sandstone, past these oak-set glens, past these fern-decked alcoves, past these mural curves, we glide hour after hour, stopping now and then as our attention is arrested by some new wonder," Powell wrote.

The splendor of the canyon has changed little

Shadows enhance the rugged forms of the canyon in the view from Point Imperial on the North Rim.

since the Powell expedition. There are still the sheer walls, tiny rills tinkling across the red stone and patches of green here and there, sprinkled in improbable places, defying gravity and the elements.

Hardy Indians wrested a livelihood from the forbidding land, but each day must have been a supreme effort. Evidence of primitive hunters 3,000 and more years old has been discovered in dry caves. Twigs were cut, split and twisted into semblances of animals, as if the ancients created them in hope they would materialize into living creatures for food.

The hunters sought more fertile lands, and in their place came the Basketmakers, followed by the Pueblo tribe and its intricate culture. They lived in the area for about 600 years and their villages are among the more than 500 Indian sites found within the confines of the 1,050-square-mile park.

Maidenhair fern and other green plants are fed by a little waterfall as it splashes down Elves' Chasm.

The Navajo and Hopi live on reservations to the east of the park while the dwindling Havasupai dwell in a small area in the western section of Grand Canyon. The 200 Havasupais, whose tribal name means "people of the blue-green water," farm a small valley irrigated by Havasu Creek.

This lush valley, with its docile, sequestered people, is in sharp contrast with much of the canyon where a forbidding desert spreads beneath the rims. The bighorn sheep has found survival difficult here, and its barren stretch has isolated on the Kaibab Plateau to the north a tiny colony of tufted-eared tree squirrels, the rare Kaibab.

South of Grand Canyon are the San Francisco Peaks, which reach 12,670 feet, the highest in Arizona. From their peaks to the depths of the canyon is a range of plant and animal life encompassing the identical varieties a traveler would find on a track from the Arctic Circle to northern Mexico, each having found its ecological niche in this relatively small section of a wild and free place.

The spectacle of the canyon from the air is indescribable; flat stretches of unbroken stone suddenly turning 90 degrees and dropping thousands of feet to the silvery knife of water appearing as a line of indolent mercury beneath the noon sun.

Within the canyon, the insignificance of man is realized with the first uplift of the eyes to rims above, dark shadows creasing the walls in the foreground and blue-hazed peaks beyond the next bend in the river. Here and there are wide places where the river's current has slowed a bit, depositing sand and silt on a narrow bank where a little green flourishes.

To those who find their greatest appreciation of the canyon from within it, rather than standing on the rims, and looking below, Theodore Roosevelt was moved to say when the century was only three years old: "In the Grand Canyon, Arizona has a natural wonder which, so far as I know, is in kind absolutely unparalleled. I want to ask you to do one thing in connection with it in your own interest and in the interest of the country — to keep this great wonder of nature as it now is. I hope you will not have a building of any kind . . . or anything else to mar the wonderful grandeur, the sublimity, the great loneliness and the beauty of the canyon. Leave it as it is. You cannot improve on it. The ages have been at work on it, and man can only mar it."

While snow falls on the rim (above), the temperature may be 50 degrees at the bottom of the canyon. Prickly pear blossoms (overleaf) bloom with the dark wall of the South Rim in the background.

The Inner Gorge of the Colorado River (left) as the late afternoon sun illuminates red limestone formations. View through an arch on the South Rim (below), the rim most often frequented by park visitors. Arizona State Highway 67 (lower right) leads visitors to the North Rim. After a passing rain storm (right), dark clouds rise above the North Rim.

*N*ine million years ago the Colorado River began to cut through land while the land slowly rose and today the mile-deep Grand Canyon exposes two billion years of geologic history (left). Its width of nine miles came from landslides which provided abrasive material to deepen the channel further. After a summer rainstorm, a rainbow bends (opposite) into the canyon passing a ponderosa pine standing on the rim.

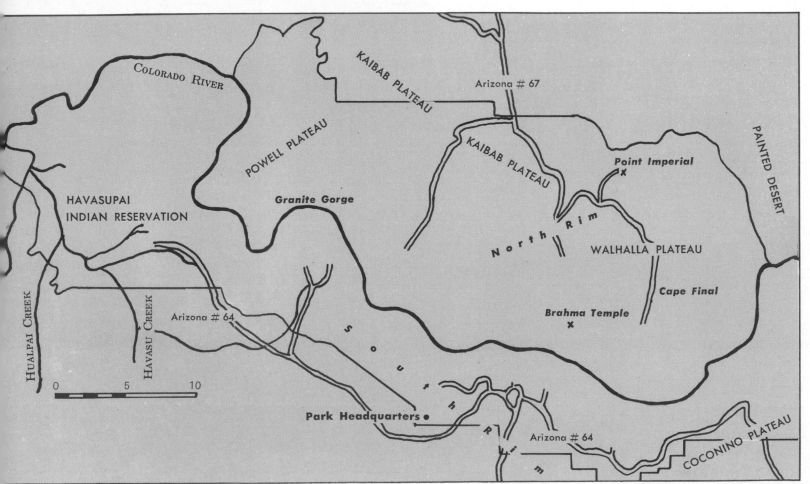

COLORADO RIVER

KAIBAB PLATEAU

Arizona # 67

KAIBAB PLATEAU

POWELL PLATEAU

PAINTED DESERT

Point Imperial
×

HAVASUPAI
INDIAN RESERVATION

Granite Gorge

North Rim

WALHALLA PLATEAU

Cape Final

Brahma Temple
×

Arizona # 64

South Rim

0   5   10

Park Headquarters ●

Arizona # 64

COCONINO PLATEAU

HUALPAI CREEK

HAVASU CREEK

GRAND CANYON NATIONAL PARK

GRAND TETON

LOCATION: Northwestern Wyoming
SIZE: 302,571 acres
ESTABLISHED: 1929

Mount Moran, reflected in Buffalo Fork of the Snake River, is flat-topped because sediment covers jagged rock beneath. The Teton's incredible peaks have drawn Indians, trappers, cattle men and tourists to this exciting, rugged land.

Vast, snow-covered graph lines of gray are etched upon the spring-breath blue of sky, mirroring their mighty heights upon apparently miniscule lakes below; giant shadows are cast across already-dark forests of deep green.

The Tetons give no hint of their ascension; no telltale foothills lead the viewer's eyes gradually to this grandiose essence of all the beauty that the mountains of the West have to offer; for here there is a glassy lake, a stand of conifers and suddenly there are those incredible peaks.

Through the great valley pours the Snake River, a wide and rushing stream flowing clearly across a deep bed of sand and stones where gamefish dart in cool depths and to which adventurous man escapes

An old whitebark pine stands on a hillside below the Grand Teton in the center of the Cathedral Group.

for a few moments to ply the current in a fragile rubber raft.

Lakes lie among the green like a cool morning's dew on a field of newly mown grain, glistening in the sun between the natural fist of the Tetons on one side and wind-whispered forests of conifers on the other. Here and there are sun-splashed meadows, a crown of green wearing the royal jewels of complacent wildflowers and streams trickling through rich, black humus where the colors of spring blooms push their way through the floor of last autumn's fallen leaves. This forest is not silent, for there is the pleasure grunt of the moose with newfound food, the chattering of thousands of birds feeding and the scrape then crash of a long-dead tree as the black bear uncovers a delicacy of insects burrowed beneath. There is the hoof of the deer as a doe leads her fawn to shoots of green ready to burst through the carpet of the forest.

The graceful mule deer pick their way down mountain trails in fall, seeking vegetation in the valleys below. High above are a few bighorn sheep, laboring among the rocks finding forage, while thousands of American elk (wapiti) move through the park in herds. In autumn, the big-chested bull elks trumpet mightily, the sound echoing and re-echoing as they lead their harems through the forest.

There are some birds here in winter, but in summer more than 200 species from bee-sized hummingbirds to eagles and soaring falcons congregate. This peaceful place even attracts the rare trumpeter swan.

Each season unfolds something new; yellow masses of buttercups spring forth shortly after the snow melts, followed by violets, spring beauties, yellow fritillary, the mariposa lily and shooting stars. Calypso orchids hide their delicate beauty in damp and dark corners, while late-blooming gentians begin to unfold as summer's heat wanes. On the peaks, where the warmth lasts but a few weeks, alpine flowers bud, blossom and go to seed in a matter of days.

The mountains are hard, crystalline rock, hugging, in part, Cascade Canyon where a trail rims beaver-built ponds and crosses meadows, skirting great slashes of boulders on hillsides. The valley of Jackson Hole is filled with rock and gravel too porous to hold water, and is therefore covered with the tenacious sagebrush, common to semidesert regions.

The Tetons' beginning was nine million years

An all day journey down the Snake River takes one past the Cathedral Group which stands over 13,000 feet above sea level. Later the river picks up speed going through narrow channels and small but exciting rapids.

ago when a chunk of earth was thrust up along the west side of Jackson Hole. The crack in the surface, Teton fault, divided the masses of rock. To the east, they sank, and to the west rose slowly. The high country formed the Tetons, then perhaps some 20,000 feet above sea level. Erosion worked upon the peaks, sending showers of rock and stone into the valley, then glaciers completed the task in the Ice Age as the sandpaper effect wore away sharp ridges, filling gorges, then water put the finishing touches on these great natural works.

The precipitous east face is what remains of the gigantic fault which began the process. Beneath it lies the valley, relatively flat and even, because of the sinking process. The lakes were holes created by glaciers, and the depressions scattered across the floor of Jackson Hole were formed when huge blocks of ice, the leavings of the glaciers, became buried. When they melted, their coverings collapsed.

The beginning of the 19th century saw the last of Indian control over the Grand Tetons. John Colter, a former member of the Lewis and Clark expedition, explored the area in 1807, the first of a line of hunters and trappers. Teton Pass was crossed by the Astorians in 1811 on their way to fortune in the Northwest. The French-Canadian trappers found their way here, naming the Grand, Middle and South

Teton mountains "Les Trois Tetons," or "The Three Breasts." The great and rugged mountain men, Jim Bridger, Jedediah Smith and David Jackson, for whom the Hole is named, lived and trapped here, reaping the bounty of valuable furs bestowed on the remote region. *The Virginian,* a classic Western novel by Owen Wister published in 1902 , did much to publicize the area.

The trappers have vanished, along with the hunters, and in their footsteps walk a new breed of adventure-seekers, the mountain climbers. The Tetons are classed by experts as among the best in the world, since there is a mountain here to match every skill from steep footpaths to sheer walls of solid granite, affording pitons a safe and secure footing. The classic climb is 13,766-foot Grand Teton which takes about two days with an overnight camp about 11,500 feet up. Other recreational attractions include boating down the Snake River, fishing in the clear blue lakes and streams and hiking the miles of trails.

Grand Teton National Park was established in 1929, and in 1950 Congress added another 52 square miles to it, the gift of John D. Rockefeller, Jr. It brought the total to about 473 square miles, a spectacular corner of the United States where nature is the great equalizer, enthralling all who reap this majestic scene with their eyes.

The Teton Range is a gigantic block in the earth's crust uplifted along a 40-mile long fault, a zone of weakness, and then carved out by glacial action.

The Episcopal Chapel of the Transfiguration (above) at Moose Entrance Station is one of many religious centers at the national parks. Jackson Lake (overleaf) at the foot of the Tetons in the central section.

*C*limbers (left) work their way up Teton Glacier on Grand Teton Mountain. The two-day strenuous climb to the summit of "The Grand" can be made only with permission from the park's Mountaineering Headquarters and never alone. Jackson Lake (above) is popular with boaters, skiers and sailors. This wide lake in Jackson Hole was formed from the waters of melted glaciers after the relatively recent Ice Age.

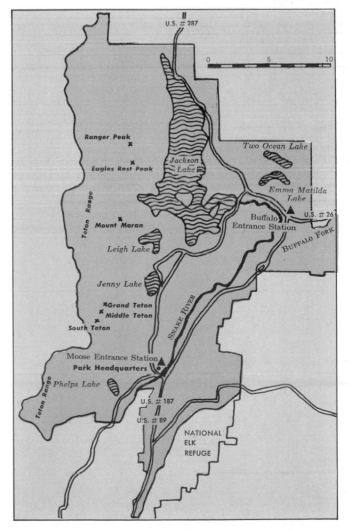

GRAND TETON NATIONAL PARK

GREAT SMOKY MOUNTAINS

LOCATION: Western North Carolina
and Eastern Tennessee
SIZE: 511,096 acres
ESTABLISHED: 1930

Rising high between the states of North Carolina and Tennessee are the Great Smoky Mountains, the highest range of the Appalachian Chain which extends from Gaspé, Canada, to northern Georgia. The lofty range of the Smokies is the climax of the Appalachians and is the backbone of Great Smoky Mountains National Park.

Known as the cradle of eastern American vegetation, this area supplied plants and animals to the land exposed for the first time in thousands of years as the glacial ice sheet retreated northward. Primeval and timeworn as they are, vegetation densely covers the Smokies with a sea of green from base to summits, some rising more than 6,000 feet.

At first, the Great Smokies may appear to have a certain sameness, then suddenly the delight unfolds: The presence of junglelike plant life together with the prevalent haze charms many who visit the park. Wisps of fog rise from the valley as low-hanging clouds roll through the gaps following the summer rainstorms when most of the precipitation falls. Blue, cold water falls into rushing streams, tipping over the edges of stone after stone. A half-light hovers at the doorway to a mysterious, beckoning cave.

The mountains are steep, but not nearly unconquerable, faced with high rock, but not having the sheer face of the Tetons. Nature has mellowed the Great Smokies with time, gently filling deep valleys and rounding sharp peaks so that they have a graceful, undulating rhythm. The harshness has been worn away and replaced with placidity.

All this took time, 880 million years of it, before the Ice Age's glacial sheet covered the central United States down to the Ohio River, destroying all that lay before them. The Great Smoky Mountains escaped the earth-gnawing glaciers since they were beyond their reach and their climate an anathema to the masses of ice.

Gravel, sand and mud deposits first covered the region, the layers compressing the ones beneath until time and weight solidified them more than three miles thick. Then the land began to rise and side pressures caused the once-solid formations to break or buckle, forming faults in the surface. This disturbance affected much of North America.

Then the ice sheet destroyed and restricted much of the vegetation and animals around the Great Smoky Mountains. The region was at first refuge, then provider, when the ice retreated to the north, furnishing plant and animal life to the land which was raped.

As life began to spread outward from what is now part of the park, the rivers came and cut channels through the land mass, creating valleys in a haphazard pattern. The ages have done the rest, wearing away

The 600 miles of streams, including Little Pigeon River, add to the gentle scenic beauty of Great Smoky.

Located south of the Cades Cove loop road, the John Oliver cabin dates from 1818, when the veteran of the War of 1812 made his way across the Great Smokies to become the area's first permanent white settler.

mountain peaks, brushing away harsh corners and filling too deep valleys with rock and silt so that vegetation might live and bring still more beauty to this ancient geological structure.

Most of the trees survived the rigorous climate to become the nucleus of deciduous trees which eventually spread and reforested the land with eastern hardwood trees.

There is no timberline; wide expanses of trees cover the hills with a mantle of green, shedding a fraction of their used vegetation each fall to build the humus for the enormous variety of flora for which the Smokies are noted.

Here are the broadleaved trees — yellow poplar, white ash, American beech, black cherry and northern red oak, growing below the mountain ash and red spruce in the cooler regions at higher altitudes. Surprisingly, the forests overlap because of environmental factors, but the spruce and fir stands are generally found in the Canadian zone above 5,000 feet.

The trees are a part of an ecological cycle existing because of the protection given the region by its national park status. Their life is interrelated with smaller plants, the rhododendron, ferns and a gamut of wildflowers. They, in turn, are links in the chain of survival for 50 species of mammals, 200 types of birds and fish hovering silently in deep stream-pools.

This country attracted settlers who were hardy, self-sufficient people mostly from Scotland and England. They vied for hunting and fishing lands with the Cherokee Indians whose reservation is now adjacent to the park on the south. The customs, speech and names of those pioneers cling to the region today.

Some of their descendants lived in Cades Cove, Tennessee, which was an isolated community until World War I and some of its citizens joined the armed services. It was seven years after the armistice before a good road linked this tiny town with the world around it. Today Cades Cove visitors can see the cabins and churches and the mill grinding corn-meal which was left when these mountain people sold their properties to the Government at the time the area became a national park.

Today, there are nearly 800 square miles for the people's pleasure in this region where all that is gentle and soft is supreme; a mass of green winter and summer, a climate kind to man, an abundant supply of water to nourish the natural treasures preserved in these venerable mountains.

Along Tennessee State Highway 73 flowers bloom in summer amid the trees that round the Great Smoky Mountains. A blue-green mist, for which the mountains were named, rises from the dense plant growth.

The fastidious raccoon begins a search for his dinner. He has his choice of over 70 kinds of fish including rainbow and brook trout.

A sunset at the 6,593-foot Mount Le Conte colors the early evening skies with a prism of color before the solitude of darkness begins.

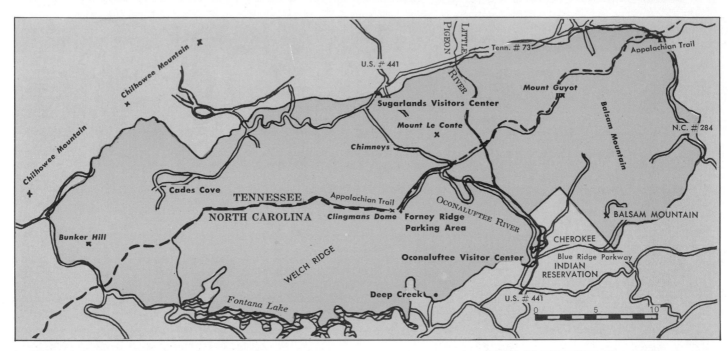

GREAT SMOKY MOUNTAINS NATIONAL PARK

*A*long the Appalachian Trail, which forms the border between Tennessee and North Carolina, is a point called Charlie's Bunion (opposite, above) commanding an excellent view of the park. The highest point of the intermountain route is Newfound Gap (opposite, below). The higher elevations in the park contain extensive stands of virgin red spruce. A rehabilitated cabin (left) is evidence of the settlers who lived quietly in this area well into the 20th century.

HALEAKALA

LOCATION: Hawaii
(Maui Island)
SIZE: 17,130 acres
ESTABLISHED: 1961

The land sleeps here now, resting under the warm Pacific sun after the long day geologists count in millions of years. To Haleakala (pronounced HA-lay-ah-kah-LA), it is night and a well-deserved rest, for this Hawaiian volcano helped form the lovely green fingers that probe the sea as part of our 50th state.

To Polynesians, it means "House of the Sun," and it was once that, belching forth angry torrents of fire and lava, making night as day, until it subsided in placid surrender to time, leaving as a heritage one of the showplaces of the National Park System so that all might understand the forces of geological evolution.

On a clear day — and there are many in the Pacific — the summit affords a spectacular view of the neighboring islands of Hawaii, Lanai, Molokai and occasionally Oahu. Turn the eyes a bit downward, and unfolding beyond the crater's rim is a vast hole in the earth, gouged by water erosion, leaving acres of symmetrical cinder cones painted with primeval colors huddled inside the great formations of cliffs whose tops are hidden in the moist clouds, lending even more vastness to the gigantic, dormant crater seven and a half miles long and two and a half miles wide.

Haleakala's history is shrouded in the still-growing science of geology, yet many scientists agree that this House of the Sun was once more than 11,000 feet high, a summit about 1,000 feet greater than the one we see now. She once slowed her volcanic eruptions,

Meaning "House of the Sun," Haleakala Crater (opposite) changes color almost hourly as the sun passes overhead, becoming most vivid at mid-afternoon. When viewed from the rim above Kapalaoa Cabin (above), hikers on the Sliding Sands Trail can see the 19-square mile crater floor 3,000 feet below the summit.

and water came to carve two deep valleys in opposite sides of the mountain which eventually met. Then, the fury of the subterranean eruptions began anew and lava flows cascaded into the valleys atop one another after their first outpourings reached the sea. The level of the valleys seen today is the height of the cooled, molten rock, save for a bit of topsoil created by time alone.

Cones of cinder were formed as high as 600 feet, and volcanic bombs and spatter spurted from fissures in the earth, propelled by supercharged gases. Eventually, a water-carved depression, one partially filled, was created, resembling a true volcanic crater. Until 1961, it was hidden by distance from the rest of Hawaii Volcanoes National Park, when it was made a singular attraction of the system because of its size.

The House of the Sun is quiet now, for no erup-tions have occurred here for centuries. But there is the appeal of something new, raw, a just-formed land, and in geological terms it is that. Lava is sterile stuff, for nothing can survive its heat. Generations of plant life have rained down upon the cooled rock until, in places, anyway, here and there a plant has been able to gain a foothold. That is fortunate, for they will flourish, then die, deepening the topsoil by a fraction of a millimeter so that other plants might follow eventually.

Life grows slowly at Haleakala National Park, for this is still a new land. But the silversword has fought grazing animals, man and the barren beds of lava to thrust its spheres of silvery, dagger-shaped leaves and three to seven-foot flowers, casting to the four winds thousands of seeds, then dying — the first handful of compost to fertilize the silent mountain.

Found nowhere else in the world, the silversword (right) grows mostly in dry cinder areas in the crater or above 8,000 feet on the outer slopes. Despite its relation to sunflowers, it resembles a yucca. Hanakauhi (below), at 8,910 feet above sea level, is part of the crater's north rim. Within Haleakala Crater there are hundreds of cinder cones (below left), formed by ash spurted through their vents.

97

HAWAII VOLCANOES

LOCATION: Hawaii
(Hawaii Island)
SIZE: 201,007 acres
ESTABLISHED: 1916

Huge mountains, their gray, lifeless sides warmed by the Pacific sun, spout their anger at the placid blue seas around them, belching fountains of lava and red fire into the sky, pouring orange-red streams of molten rock down unresisting slopes.

This is a link with the past; geological history in the making as the Hawaiian Islands continue to emerge from the sea as they first did five to ten million years ago. Hawaii Island, largest of the chain, is the site of Mauna Loa, a 13,680-foot summit where Hawaii Volcanoes National Park begins, stretching southeast to the seacoast, a place of contrasts where umbrella-shaped palms and dense jungles of ferns lie near gaunt mountains and beside lava deserts.

The region has fascinated visitors for more than a century. The Rev. William Ellis, a British missionary, saw it in 1823 and said in his *A Tour Through Hawaii:* ". . . A spectacle, sublime and even appalling, presented itself before us. We stopped and trembled. Astonishment and awe for some moments rendered us mute. . . . The bottom was covered with lava, and the southwest and northern parts of it were one vast flood of burning matter, in a stage of terrific ebullition, rolling to and fro its 'fiery surge' and flaming billows."

The spectacle of the volcano, Kilauea, impressed Mr. Ellis and countless thousands since. Within the volcano at that time, at Halemaumau, was a great lake of rolling lava which spread across the floor, and

Effervescing several hundred feet, the lava fountain (left) is considered to be relatively gentle. Hawaii Volcanoes National Park has two of the most active volcanoes in the world. Restricted to the volcanic mountains of Hawaii Island is the rare Néné' or Hawaiian Goose (above), which is now on the verge of extinction.

at other times seeped into earth fissures to produce avalanches of fire. A later visitor stared at the sight, then told a guide, "I've seen hell. Now I want to go home." This "lava-lake" phase ceased with the steam explosion of 1924.

From the 11-mile Crater Rim Drive around the summit caldera of Kilauea volcano, Kilauea Crater, the visitor can see the destruction wrought by the forces of nature — cones of cinder, bluffs alive with steam and recent flows of lava. One of the most impressive sections is the "devastated area," which was denuded of vegetation during the 1959 eruption of Kilauea Iki. The ancient Hawaiians made a deity of Pele, the goddess of volcanoes, whom they believed lived in Halemaumau, Kilauea's most active vent. It was her wrath, they said, which caused the eruptions, destroying villages and tilled lands.

From the summit caldera, the visitor passes along the Chain of Craters, part of the east rift of the volcano where the road winds past deep craters in which eruptions have recently taken place. In March, 1965, a fissure on the side of Makaopuhi Crater poured forth a lake of lava almost 300 feet deep. During the 1959 eruption of Kilauea Iki, lava spewed more than 1,900 feet high, filling a crater with molten lava to a depth of about 400 feet. Until recently, the most spectacular of all volcanoes here was Mauna Loa, but it has not erupted since 1950.

From Makaopuhi Crater near the end of the chain, the island's newest scenic road passes along the southeast coast, past ancient villages and sites of religious temples. The mighty mountains of fire must have prompted these peoples to great religious fervor. At Wahaula Heiau near the eastern edge of the park is one of the island's best-known places of worship where it is reputed that one of the last human sacrifices was performed under the old religion.

Now the religion is appreciation of and humility before nature, which is protected within the boundaries of this park in a subtropical corner of paradise.

*T*he Gingerlily (bottom) is the flower used in leis in the Hawaiian Islands. Originally from India, it is the most romantic of the gingers, with petals like folded moth wings, and sometimes grows as high as seven feet. Small lava fountains (top) in a sea of molten lava are believed to begin 35 miles down within the earth's mantle. After filling a reservoir two miles beneath the surface, the lava works its way through fissures to erupt for as long as a month at the summit. In 1959 one fountain roared at 1,900 feet, highest ever witnessed, filling Kilauea Iki (right) 400 feet deep. Cool at the surface, it remains hot beneath.

Although Hot Springs National Park is famous for its medicinal waters, it has other attractions such as interesting scenery, horseback riding and camping.

HOT SPRINGS

LOCATION: Southwest-Central Arkansas
SIZE: 1,035 acres
ESTABLISHED: 1921

A few months before he died, Hernando de Soto, bold Spanish explorer and conquistador, passed through what is now Hot Springs and possibly bathed in its waters. He was searching for gold and he probably never got closer to his impossible dream than his immersion in the warm water which springs from vents in the gray, volcanic tuff at the base of Hot Springs Mountain near the center of Arkansas.

That was the year 1541. Before the arrival of the white man the Indian was reportedly attracted to these hot waters where the "Great Spirit" dwelled. The Dunbar and Hunter Expedition in 1804 mapped the water route from Natchez to the springs and made a chemical analysis of them. Soon after, a permanent settlement developed which by 1820 included an inn and several crude canvas-shack bathhouses. In 1832 Congress set aside the hot springs as a reservation, but without supervision for over 40 years.

Today's national park of 1,035 acres is visited annually by several hundred thousand tourists. The park's primary significance is probably that it is this country's most important example of man's centuries-old romance with and affinity for the thermal and mineral waters of the world. The magical liquid minerals boil and bubble up from the west slope at the base of Hot Springs Mountain in 47 springs with an average daily flow of almost a million gallons and an average temperature of 143 degrees Fahrenheit.

"The springs are now the property of the people," the superintendent of Government bathhouses wrote to the Secretary of the Interior in 1915. "They are

free from monopoly and extortion, and within the reach of all." Yet the area did not become a national park until 1921.

There is no certainty about what causes the hot springs. The currently favored theory is that the springs are formed when rainwater sinks into the ground between Sugarloaf and West Mountains, then rises along tilted layers of rock to emerge finally through the geological fault at the base of Hot Springs Mountain.

The heated water is variously attributed to inordinately deep and uncooled underground rock, chemical reactions near the bottom of the wells, friction from sliding rock masses at profound earth-depths or compression from overlying rock burden and radioactive minerals far beyond the range of the discerning instruments of geologists.

Not all visitors take the waters. Below the mountain is the gay winter resort city of Hot Springs where horse racing and golfing rival the waters. And in the park itself, one of the nation's oldest national preserves, are five rugged little mountains and oak-hickory-pine forests which consistently bring their own special rewards.

Perhaps the late President John F. Kennedy best summed up the twin beneficence of a preserve like Hot Springs when he declared in 1962: "We must have places where we can find release from the tensions of an increasingly industrialized civilization, where we can have personal contact with the natural environment which sustains us."

There is no certain explanation of the hot springs' mechanism, but the favored theory says the water is seeping rainwater, shown as icicles at Dripping Springs.

To show visitors what the springs looked like in a natural state, one of the 47 has been left open. The others are sealed to prevent outside contamination.

Two of the many moods of Isle Royale: (above) a tranquil beauty descends with night upon the numerous lakes and islands of the archipelago, while (right) man can find himself the isolated splendor that comes with being in the north woods, away from the mainland's daily routine of hurry and heaviness.

ISLE ROYALE

LOCATION: Michigan
(in Lake Superior)
SIZE: 539,347 acres
ESTABLISHED: 1940

Isle Royale, now north woods wilderness held in a lake's solitude, is visibly haunted by the grace and majesty of its geologic past. This handsomely endowed protectorate of vast Lake Superior, in Michigan, and 22 miles from the Minnesota shore, is enveloped by the greatest of the Great Lakes, the lake which marks the site of the southern end of an ancient and possibly one of the highest mountain ranges that ever existed on our continent.

The formation of Lake Superior and perhaps Isle Royale itself is explained eloquently by Rutherford Platt in *The Great American Forest:* "Through timeless eras . . . in many places the uplift of mountains so weakened the edge of the Canadian Shield [a shield is a broad, massive, symmetrical rock upheaval] that it gave way, . . . creating depressions for future lakes and river valleys."

The pure copper deposits of Isle Royale and even the mineral riches of its geologic cousin the Mesabi Range are explained by Platt: "The Canadian Shield became the pedestal of the North Woods." He describes the intrusions of plutonic minerals and the ravaging of the area's surface by glaciers, the outcroppings of rock in which, on Isle Royale itself, the Indians found copper "so pure it can be used without smelting. This was the source of copper for Indian artifacts found scattered far and wide through the American wilderness."

Isle Royale, 45 miles in length, is redolent with the ancient history of Indian copper miners, who reportedly worked there 4,000 years ago. Its fjord-like harbors, sheltered bays and interior, parallel ridges attaining a height of 700 feet, were first looked upon by white men in 1699. These were heroic French explorers who named the island for Louis XIV.

Yet white men did not recognize that although the copper of Isle Royale was satisfactory for the primitive artisan, it wasn't in sufficient concentration for modern industrial needs. Miners ventured across the lake in the 1840's and 1870's, but by 1900 their mines were abandoned.

The canoe yielded to the motor launch, the small boat to the excursion vessel. Hotels and summer homes were beginning to multiply. A cry was raised and the administration of the second great conservationist Roosevelt responded to their reasoned pleas. In 1936, Franklin Delano Roosevelt signed the Isle Royale National Park Act resulting in its establishment four years later.

Two hundred tiny islands and countless rocks, inviting water explorers, surround the main island; thus the entire park area can be called an archipelago. A coniferous sweep of trees covers the northeast and perimeter of the island, and maple-birch hardwoods dominate the higher interior. Bald ridges, bogs, spruce and cedar swamps dot the landscape, offering additional havens for the water birds.

"The muzzles of moose cut sliding V's on the mirrors of the ponds," as Rutherford Platt suggests of the north woods area. On Isle Royale approximately 600 of the long-legged, antlered beasts form the relatively large population.

Beavers, red foxes, snowshoe hares, red squirrels find refuge and sustenance here. The lonely cry of the loon, the din of the herring gull, the scream of the bald eagle are heard on the island reaches.

There are no roads on the island. The hiker and canoeist, however, can maneuver here with more than 120 miles of trails to be negotiated amid the wild splendor, although they should remember that the nights are cool and even day temperatures seldom rise above 80 degrees. Many small boats are handy to the seeker of water worlds at Rock Harbor and Windigo. Fishermen call the island "the pike capital of the nation" because of the abundance of pike in the 200 lakes and ponds. Isle Royale is the north woods in autonomous compactness, with fascination for all.

*M*oose (left), while common at Isle Royale, did not come until 1912 when Lake Superior froze across to Canada, 15 miles away. They eat water plants, leaves and twigs. At the Middle Islands Entrance to Rock Harbor stands the Old Rock Harbor Lighthouse (above). Rock Harbor, longest of the four main harbors, is typical of the primitive, but exciting American scenery found at Isle Royale (upper right). Very common to Isle Royale is the largest rodent in the United States, the beaver (lower right). The beaver is the engineer of the wild, the only mammal, beside humans, that alters its environment to suit its needs. Most active at dusk and dawn, the beaver builds and repairs dams, lodges and canals.

LASSEN VOLCANIC

LOCATION: Northeastern California
SIZE: 106,127 acres
ESTABLISHED: 1916

Lassen Peak, reflected in a nearby lake, stands at the southern end of the Cascade Range. The largest plug dome volcano in the world dominates the park, a park that offers both scenic beauty and geologic interest because of its extensive volcanic past.

In the order of nature, often where there is chaos, great beauty is nearby.

This seems to be particularly true of the lush, sylvan beauty that neighbors on volcanoes in Italy, the South Sea Islands, South America and, in our own country, Lassen Volcanic National Park of northeastern California. For where volcanoes are, active or inactive, the slopes and lowlands of the tumultuous mountains are usually rich with the resources that satisfy the physical and spiritual needs of man: food and drink for his body, shelter for his family.

Lassen Peak, once called San Jose by Spanish explorers, is now an inactive plug dome volcano. But it was once considered the only active volcano in the United States, having erupted as recently as 1914 and 1915, remaining fire-breathing and occasionally rumbling until 1921.

The 10,457-foot peak was the habitat and wonderment of four tribes of Indians long before Spaniard Luis Arguillo discovered it in 1821. This once fierce, lava-spewing mountain in the Cascade Range, not far from the Sierra Nevada, served as a territorial monument, dividing the regions of the Atsugewi, Maidu, Yana and Yahi, who foraged in its vicinity and lived in harmony around its slopes. In the park, also, the true American natives must have known the fearsome majesty of other volcanic heights now called Cinder Cone, Bumpass Hell and Devils Kitchen.

Now, as then, coniferous forests, flower-blanketed mountain meadows, sun-glinting and tree-shadowy lakes and streams characterize the 165 square mile area. Deer are abundant in the fields of summer; over 150 species of birds beautify the foliage; golden-mantled ground squirrels, chipmunks, red squirrels, bear are permanent tenants.

The view from Lassen Park Road, extending from the southwestern to northwestern corner of the park,

Lassen Park Road (California 89) meanders past the major interest sites of Lassen Volcanic National Park.

110

and half encircling the base of Lassen Peak, is stunningly comprehensive. Yet the leisurely assimilation of the park's beauty and bizarre landmarks appeals more to the view from behind a walking stick than through an automobile windshield. It is a hiker's and camper's park, demanding the effort, and offering scenic rewards not accessible to the automobile. The 150 miles of trails are highlighted by the path which leads to Bumpass Hell, a 16-acre tract of boiling, sulphurous springs, named after K. V. Bumpass who discovered it in 1864.

The peak, the park, the surrounding national forest and a county, all are named after Peter Lassen, a Danish immigrant blacksmith, who familiarized himself and others with the area in the 1830's. He early acquired a large parcel of land at Vina, California. During the Gold Rush he guided migrants across these mountains from the East, into the Sacramento Valley. He used the peak as a storied landmark and his rancho as a hostel. Thus, the bestowal of his name on specific points and general area, by the U.S. Geographic Board in 1915.

Lassen's trail, however, did not wind into the area now included in the park. W. H. Nobles crossed through the northern part of the present expanse from Butte Lake to Manzanita Lake in 1852. Nobles' route was considered a more direct approach to the Sacramento Valley.

Lassen Peak and Cinder Cone were designated as national monuments on May 6, 1907. The eruptions in 1914 and 1915 electrified public interest in the American volcano and expedited the park's establishment on August 9, 1916. Here is a park and peak which Associate Supreme Court Justice, William O. Douglas, must have had in mind when he wrote that some people "must find a peak or a ridge that they can reach under their own power alone."

Bumpass Hell, where steam rises from boiling mudpots, indicates that Lassen may be dormant but not extinct.

MAMMOTH CAVE

The darkness grips the visitor, then the depths slowly come into focus as the eyes adjust themselves to the underworld of Kentucky's Mammoth Cave, which has been a lure to awestruck men since it was first trod by primitives.

It is still a place of mystery, this partially unexplored hollow land beneath the surface. The ancients braved superstition and penetrated more than three miles of its vaulted passages, seeking gypsum. The dry, even temperatured air has preserved for centuries their worn-out sandals and burnt torch ends, scattered here and there among footprints before sheer walls hacked with rude stone tools. Why they sought the soft mineral is not known. The remains of one of them is still there, his body mummified after he was crushed by a six-ton boulder while gathering the stone 2,400 years ago.

The yawning cavern was rediscovered by an unknown white man in 1798, and a few years later by another seeking saltpeter, or potassium nitrate, a prime ingredient of black gunpowder. The bored-out tree trunks used to carry the chemical solution to vats are still here, along with other well-preserved artifacts of the operation.

The saltpeter industry died after the War of 1812; then began Mammoth Cave's career as a tourist attraction, although much of it remained unexplored. Jenny Lind sang here, her voice echoing and reechoing through the rooms of stone. Edwin Booth, the great Shakespearian actor, intoned the philosophy of Hamlet in this apt surrounding and Grand Duke Alexis of Russia paid the cave a visit along with thousands of others who linked it with Niagara Falls as a great attraction.

In 1837 a 15-year-old boy named Stephen Bishop, among the cave's first guides, crossed the Bottomless Pit on a slender pole, opening the way to extensive uncharted corridors and passages. Bishop guided the many eminent scientists who visited the cave there-

LOCATION: Southwest-Central Kentucky
SIZE: 51,351 acres
ESTABLISHED: 1941

Iron oxide in the calcium carbonate gives the Golden Fleece (left) in Mammoth Cave its golden color. The Hindu Temple (above) displays many varied cave formations: stalactites, stalagmites and columns.

after, and achieved world renown before he died in 1859. He is buried in what is now the park. Later the cave became an underground tuberculosis sanitarium. It was proposed as a national park in 1911, but that wasn't accomplished until 30 years later.

The cave is a maze of corridors connecting huge, domed chambers and deep pits. They were formed 340 million years ago when the limestone was the bed of an ancient sea. The land rose, and water inched into the rock, eroding the giant passages seen today. The formations have quaint, picturesque names — Fat Man's Misery, a narrow channel out into the floor of a large room; Frozen Niagara; the Snowball Room. Among the half-dozen guided tours available in Mammoth Cave is a boat ride on Echo River, the world's best-known underground stream. Nearly a million persons a year visit this great natural wonder.

Above ground, two lovely rivers flow through the park, winding past deep green forests and a blaze of colorful wildflowers, a strange paradox to the weird, wonderful world spread out, down below.

114

Blindfish (left), which inhabit the subterranean Echo River, have developed acute senses of touch and smell. They are small, colorless and translucent. Stalactites and stalagmites form rigid columns in the Lion's Cage (above left). During the War of 1812, the Rotunda (above) was used to mine saltpeter. This huge room is one of Mammoth Cave's largest. Onyx stalactites combine to make the Drapery Room, a popular sight at Mammoth Cave National Park.

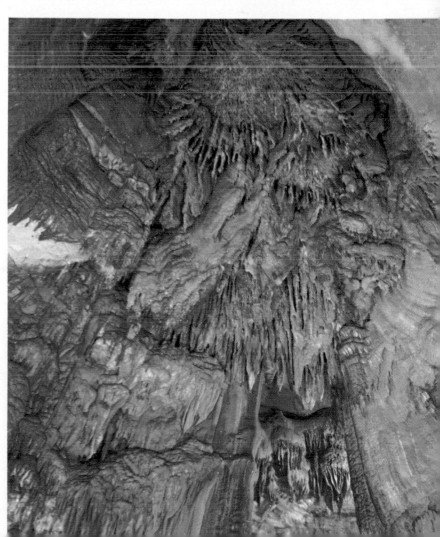

MESA VERDE

LOCATION: Southwestern Colorado
SIZE: 51,277 acres
ESTABLISHED: 1906

About 250 years before conquistador Coronado's ruthless and romanticized quest in 1540 through Arizona and New Mexico, seeking the illusory wealth of the "Seven Cities of Cibola," the cliff-dwelling Indians of southwestern Colorado's Mesa Verde had disappeared into archeological history.

For 800 years the Indians of the Four Corners country cultivated their beans and maize, lived and prospered — then vanished.

The empty homes of these departed people remain behind today, preserved in protective rock-shelters by the mild climate of this country. Those who come today to wonder at the majesty of Cliff Palace, the largest cliff dwelling of them all, must feel much as the cowboys did in the late 19th century when they stumbled onto it while looking for grazing cattle from atop the mesa.

News of the discoveries spread rapidly, and before long a great many curious people began to wander among the ruins, ferreting out their secrets. Unfortunately these people included careless tourists and callous curio-seekers, and some serious damage to the ruins resulted. Even though this was not an altogether bright period in the history of the Mesa Verde, the work of these early explorers began to attract the attention of more serious scholars. One of these was Gustaf Nordenskiold, a Swedish scientist who in 1891 directed the first scientific excavations in several of the cliff dwellings and published his findings. By 1900 a women's organization, the Colorado Cliff Dwellings Association, was incorporated and began working for the preservation of the ancient buildings. In 1906 their efforts attained fruition and Mesa Verde National Park was established by act of Congress on June 29. One result of this act is a regulation stating that all visitors to cliff dwellings must be accompanied by a National Park Service employee.

So successful has been the excavation and repair of the early damage to these precipitous Indian mansions that Cliff Palace, Balcony House and Spruce Tree House are now considered to be the best examples of cliff dwellings to be found in the continental United States. These citadels of man, built like the eagle's aerie in inaccessibility to enemy attack from below, are an everlasting tribute to how primitive man mastered the enduring craft of masonry.

In the Mesa Verde museum are restored fragile artifacts of cookery, agriculture, jewelry and pottery

The imposing Square Tower House (right), dating from the 11th century, was discovered by settlers in 1888.

which tell the history of a vanished cliff-dwelling civilization in graphic detail.

Although the story of Indian life on the Mesa Verde has been preserved so clearly, the sudden departure of these people from their homeland remains a mystery. As one gazes at the cliff dwellings, perched in the cliffs high above the canyon floors, they may seem to him impregnable castles, often guarded by towers. Perhaps a persistent enemy finally overran the farmers of the mesa, but there are other possibilities. The narrower growth of tree-rings in the late 13th century suggests to some that drought may have driven the Indians from this region. It may be that after 800 years of farming the mesa tops the Indians had exhausted the soils. Nevertheless the visitor who lets his imagination play over the spectacle of the cliff houses generally departs with a memory of the defensive refuges of a harassed people.

The quest for clues to these ancient people continues. The mystery may soon be solved in concrete scientific analysis. The National Park Service recently completed a five-year archeological study of Wetherill Mesa in the undeveloped western section of the park and possibly will come up with certain key answers.

When the new area under study is opened to the public, the number of cliff dwellings accessible to tourists, archeologists and anthropologists will double. Long House, Mug House and Step House specifically will be added to the park's houses of ancient wonder. And a new museum on Wetherill Mesa will fill out the gradually focusing jigsaw puzzle which gives us a quaint, unique, historical picture of a vanished American people.

The 400,000 people who visit Mesa Verde annually are thus given an extraordinary opportunity to be grateful for the forces of preservation and conservation which enable them to reflect on both the intrinsic perishability and immortality which is the life and time of man.

Shadows move across Mesa Verde plateau country (right) as 9,884-foot Ute Peak stands snowcapped in the distance. The Sun Temple (opposite, above), a mesa-top ceremonial structure, was built about 1200 A.D. near Fewkes Canyon. Under summer clouds, the La Plata Mountains provide a background for scenic views along Mesa Verde park road (opposite, below).

Ancient masonry forms are viewed through a doorway at Spruce Tree House (below left), the best preserved large cliff dwelling. A diorama of Spruce Tree House (left) in the park museum depicts the daily life of the Pueblo villagers. The Cliff Palace (below) is the most extensive of the park's cliff dwellings. The circular ceremonial chambers near the living areas were central features of the Pueblo culture.

MOUNT McKINLEY

The Wilderness of Denali is not tamed. It is raw and primal, and a man feels very small in it. Almost anywhere off the one road he is truly alone — and sometimes a little afraid.

It is a vast land, which dwarfs normal scales. Sprawling river bars, peopled with the swarming specks that are the caribou, wind out of immensity at the foot of the hills. The wind across the tundra is clean, untainted by mankind.

The spirit of the wolf hangs over the land. Unseen, his presence is felt. He is the warden and unwitting benefactor of the caribou, the superb culmination of the biotic pyramid — and the personification of the wild.

Over all, the Alaska Range rises in a succession of brilliant ridges, cornices, peaks — each magnificent in its own right, but nearly lost in the greater picture. Higher they rise, leading the eye to the massive upsurge that is *The Mountain*. A full three vertical miles above the living tundra soars its peak.

Nothing lives on the mountain, but the mountain lives. Avalanches leap from its walls. Seracs crash; glaciers rumble and grind. Clouds swirl about its flanks, and a snow plume is torn by the wind from its uppermost crests. In the evening, the glare of the eternal ice softens, glows with the color of fireweed, then pales to ivory against the darkened sky.

No one knows what white man saw the country first. Russian traders knew the mountain, called it *Bulshaia Gora,* or "Big Mountain." Early prospectors knew it as Densmore's Mountain. The Indians of the area had perhaps the most beautiful and fitting name of all: "Denali," "The High One."

But it was a young prospector, W. A. Dickey, who

LOCATION: South-Central Alaska
SIZE: 1,939,493 acres
ESTABLISHED: 1917

A subarctic wilderness at summer sunset (opposite): Wonder Lake and Mount McKinley, which at 20,320 feet is North America's highest peak. It is 250 miles south of Arctic Circle. Caribou (above), which are seen along the park road, are unique to Mount McKinley in the park system.

Among the park's many mountain glaciers is Muldrow Glacier. Some glaciers are 30 to 40 miles long.

realized the importance of the 20,320-foot peak in 1896, and named it after the champion of the gold standard, President William McKinley.

It is fortunate that one of the earliest explorers of the area was a naturalist and conservationist. Charles Sheldon, hunting specimens for the National Museum, roamed the country for three years, and felt its impact. Recognizing the intrinsic value of the landscape and its wildlife, he conceived the idea of making the area a national park while camping there in the summer of 1906. His vigorous efforts to create a refuge for the swarming wildlife, aided by the Boone and Crockett Club, brought about the establishment of Mount McKinley National Park just eleven years later. Today it is the only Park Service area which harbors the white Dall sheep and the barren grounds caribou, and its 3,030 square miles

embrace more untouched wilderness than any other national park.

Mountaineers answered the challenge of Mount McKinley early. On April 6, 1910, a hardy group of sourdoughs climbed to the summit of the north peak of McKinley, carrying with them a 14-foot spruce pole. It was an astonishing feat, for the group was inexperienced and poorly equipped. Modern mountaineers find the climb as dangerous and demanding as a Himalayan expedition, but each year a few manage to stand atop the continent.

Relatively little has changed since Sheldon fought to make this area a park. A single graveled road winds its leisurely way 86 miles into the park, climbing from the deep green spruce of the taiga to the sweeping tapestry of the alpine tundra. You may see from the road the same wild peaks and teeming wildlife that

The Teklanika River flows down from the Alaska Range through a broad gravel bed near park road.

thrilled the first visitors. Over the tundra range groups of caribou, the bulls in late summer bearing brilliant white capes and towering, blood-red antlers. Moose, looking shiny black at a little distance, feed knee-deep in ponds or browse in willow thickets.

The deceptively lethargic-looking grizzly keeps his head down, gobbling berries, roots and grasses. Red foxes trot across the road, seemingly indifferent to man. Ptarmigan erupt into the air with a humorous, guttural croaking, their white wings flashing in startling contrast to their barred brown bodies.

In the ponds everywhere beavers are busy cutting willow. Golden eagles soar above. Gyrfalcons are sometimes seen, and marsh hawks swoop low across the dry flats. On the lower peaks, a spray of white dots becomes a flock of Dall sheep.

If you are very lucky, you may see a wolf. When you have seen the eyes of the wolf, you have seen the quintessence of wildness.

The park is generally accessible from June through the middle of September. In June and July the area is confronted with one of its few disadvantages — mosquitoes, which come after the late spring that leaves patches of snow at lower elevations even into June. During these same months there are 18 hours of sunlight daily and only semidarkness in the remaining hours. Although the winters are cold, snow depths seldom exceed three feet on the level at lower elevations.

Whatever the season, the mountain, once seen, even if its persistent shroud of clouds allows only a momentary view, becomes an indelible recollection. The wildness of the park, once experienced, even if at some distance, leaves its mark on a man.

MOUNT RAINIER

LOCATION: West-Central Washington
SIZE: 241,781 acres
ESTABLISHED: 1899

A rocky hiking trail winding up Pinnacle Peak offers a dramatic view of 14,410-foot Mount Rainier. Below the cloud line, the massive ice of the Nisqually Glacier inches slowly through a valley near Paradise, a mile-high visitor recreation area.

Rainier stands like a silent sentinel over the Cascade Range, a color covering of blue and green and tones of gray, clad in the white cap of cold and age, a garment which belies its fiery parentage.

The mountain soars above the Cascade Mountains of west-central Washington, rising 14,410 feet above sea level, her size so ponderous she covers a quarter of the national park's almost 380 square miles.

Deep, green stands of trees, alpine lakes, the diamond-tipped rush of icy water crashing over smooth boulders, delicate flowers hidden in shady glens, sprawling wild flower meadows — all are subdued by the spectacle of ice, laced like a child's finger painting across the faces of Mount Rainier. It has the greatest expanse of glaciers — about 40 in number — found in the United States outside of Alaska.

Rainier, part of that once-spectacular circle of volcanic activity which rings the Pacific from the Americas to Asia, was not always so placid, so gently touched or so green. Volcanic eruptions flowed lava upon lava, cinders upon ash, until the mountain grew with a fury nuclear energy cannot match. The Cascades to the east were created in the same manner, but Rainier retains more than a casual birthmark. At the summit are three peaks; Columbia Crest to the east is the highest, then two smaller but obvious volcanic craters. The summit craters on Columbia Crest, the mountain's high point, retain small vents which whisper steam into the thin air, melting the snow which lies about.

Now Rainier is quiet. Time, water and glaciers have worn great canyons and raised ridges along its once-smooth sides, and glaciers now spread across its body, square mile after square mile of slowly flowing ice, an active reminder of the natural forces which helped shape much of our landscape today.

One of them, the Emmons, measures over four miles long and a mile wide, built as the others by the incessant falls of snow, as much as 50 feet a year, packing layers upon layers until it is compressed by its own weight and begins to slide slowly downward. The water melts as it reaches lower elevations, but above, the tail of the glacier is always being formed so that the rushing rivers and stone-pounding streams below might have strength forever.

The water is the beginning of the various forms of natural life, irrigating lowland forests and alpine meadows. Douglas firs, western hemlocks and red cedars tower above the brown-needled floor where beams of sunlight break through and give life to Oregon grape, western sword fern, bunchberry, dogwood and soft, green mosses.

Beyond the forests lie patches of green meadows, threaded by foot trails and sprinkled with a rolling panorama of wild flowers: the avalanche fawnlily, yellow lambstongue fawnlily, western pasqueflower, marshmarigold and mountain buttercup bursting into bloom with the last snow melting. The Indian paintbrush, spikes of lupines, speedwell, valerian and American bistort fill the voids in August when the seeds of the spring flowers have been sown by the four winds to bloom again another year.

Apparently oblivious to Mount Rainier are the birds, 130 species of them, and half a hundred mammals — mule deer, black bear, elk and mountain goat, raccoons, squirrels and chipmunks — feeding in this horn of quiet plenty.

High above are plants stunted by the cold and elevation, grasping rocks and their roots seeking paper-thin fissures that nourishment might be found. The visitor here has taken a botanical "trip" far into Canada, for Hudson Bay is where this flora is generally displayed.

The snow which feeds Mount Rainier's glaciers originates as clouds over the Pacific Ocean. As the moisture-laden, westerly winds move inland, the first barrier they meet is the Cascade Range. Rising to pass over the mountains, they are cooled, and the condensing moisture falls as rain and snow. The heaviest precipitation falls on the windward slope, especially between 5,000 and 10,000 feet. Paradise Park receives about 100 inches in a year.

For all its beauty, Rainier must have been a forbidding scene to the Indians, since none of the dozen nations that visited the region is believed to have established permanent settlements. The mountain, an object of worship to some, was a hunting ground for others.

While some of the early tribes — the Nisqually, Cowlitz, Yakima and Klickitat — picked berries here in summer months, most probably feared the mountain. The deity who sent fire and molten rock through the top of a mountain was an unfriendly being, as early explorers seeking guides soon found.

Captain George Vancouver of the Royal Navy is

The nature-sculptured ice caves under the Paradise Glacier are known for their glistening illumination.

thought to be the first white man to see the mountain. On May 8, 1792, while on a journey of exploration for the British government, he wrote: "The weather was serene and pleasant, and the country continued to exhibit between us and the eastern snowy range the same luxuriant appearance. At its northern extremity, Mount Baker bore by compass North 22 East; the round, snowy mountain, now forming its southern extremity and which, after my friend, Rear Admiral Rainier, I distinguished by the name of Mount Rainier. . . ."

Tolmie Peak was named for the young Scots physician, William Fraser Tolmie, employed by Hudson Bay Company, who left Fort Nisqually in August, 1833. A few days later he climbed to the "summit of a snowy peak immediately under Mount Rainier."

It was later christened for him. Dr. Tolmie's name is also found in a creek and in the Tolmie saxifrage, a common plant growing in the park's upper regions.

Rainier itself stood unconquered for years. The first attempt in 1857 failed, and it was not until August 17, 1870, that Hazard Stevens and P. B. Van Trump reached the summit. Thirteen years later, James Longmire developed a small part of what is now the park after he discovered mineral springs.

Clouds and fog often obscure the mountain. There is, however, usually warm, clear weather from about July 1 to mid-September. In many years, Indian summer weather continues well into October, when autumn colors bring out still another kind of quality possesed by this magnificent mountain and the land that surrounds it.

*M*ount Rainier (above) stands between layers of pale color at dusk. Moisture laden clouds sweep in from the Pacific Ocean in changing patterns over the mountain. Among the many wildflowers in the park is the western anemone (right), a perennial herb found in mountain valleys. Green fir tree spires (far right) rise from the forest floor at Eunice Lake, near Tolmie Peak in the park's northwestern corner.

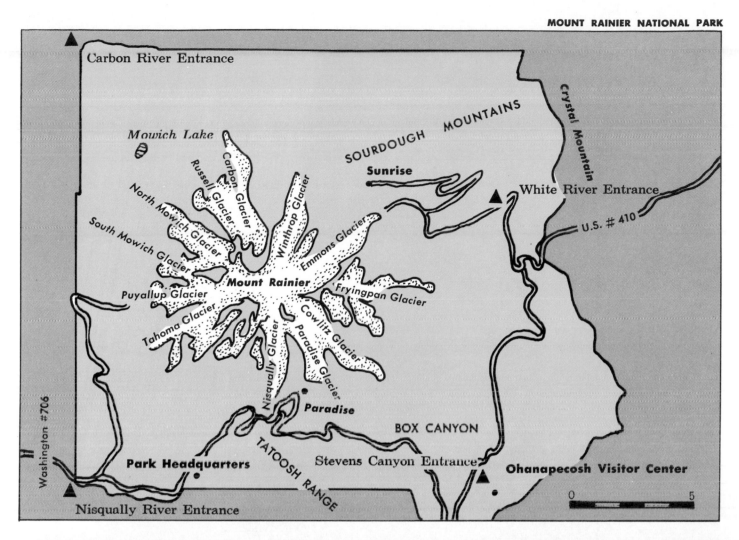

Carbon River Entrance

Mowich Lake

Russell Glacier

Carbon Glacier

North Mowich Glacier

South Mowich Glacier

Winthrop Glacier

SOURDOUGH MOUNTAINS

Sunrise

Crystal Mountain

White River Entrance

Emmons Glacier

U.S. # 410

Puyallup Glacier

Mount Rainier

Fryingpan Glacier

Tahoma Glacier

Cowlitz Glacier

Nisqually Glacier

Paradise Glacier

Paradise

BOX CANYON

Washington #706

TATOOSH RANGE

Stevens Canyon Entrance

Ohanapecosh Visitor Center

Park Headquarters

Nisqually River Entrance

0   5

*G*lacial movement, heavy snowfall and swirling winds create a changing terrain for mountaineers and skiers. A ski-climbing party passes a Camp Muir marker (opposite, below) as the sun silhouettes Mount Adams in the distance. Alpine snowfields (opposite, above) erode into low ridges under a sharp, carving wind. Ice breakups on Cowlitz Glacier (above left) and a sheer cliff face on Pinnacle Peak (above right) provide a challenge for climbers. From Sunrise (overleaf), the mountain looms skyward.

At Olympic National Park, in Washington, the civilization of man defers almost totally to the civilization of the tree. Amid these thousands of acres of mountain and coastal wilderness, 50 miles wide and 200 miles in circumference, the tropical-like luxuriance of rain forests vies in beauty and splendor with the majestic eminence of an immense conifer empire on primeval coasts and on the flanks of soaring peaks.

Such is man's deferment to this almost preternatural infinitude of green — the hushed, eternal realm of the Sitka spruce, western hemlock, Douglas-fir and red cedar, among others — that park trail crews often cut narrow, wandering foot trails through the wilderness. In the forest depths abound the natural civilization of wildlife and wildflowers — the animals, birds, and both familiar and exotic blooms, which flourish in a protective privacy redolent of the legendary preserves of Adam and Eve.

Fifty-six species of wild mammals inhabit Olympic Park, with some of their more migratory marine members ranging from season to season along the coastline from Alaska, through British Columbia and Washington State, to Lower California, over a distance of 4,000 miles. Around 6,000 "Roosevelt" elk (also called American elk or wapiti) live in the park and can be glimpsed moving toward the high country in the summer. More prominent residents also include the black-tailed deer and Olympic marmot, with mountain goat, bear, raccoons, mink, otter and mountain beaver quick and alive to the alert glance of the amateur naturalist. About 140 kinds of birds await the reverence and keen eye of the "watchers" with eagles, ravens, hawks, more discernible along the wild seacoast and among the craggy heights of the park.

Riots of wildflowers carpet the alpine meadows around Mt. Olympus, 7,965 feet high, and the other peaks, several of which rise above 7,000 feet. Of Olympic Park's wildflower life E. B. Webster said in his book, *The Friendly Mountain:* "Flowers of every shape and hue. Flowers standing shoulder to shoulder, as thick as daisies in a pasture, or clover in the field. Red columbine, yellow and blue asters, scarlet paint brushes, blue lupine, white valerian . . . all thrown

OLYMPIC

LOCATION: Northwestern Washington
SIZE: 888,558 acres
ESTABLISHED: 1938

Olympic presents two distinct topographical faces to the visitor, glacier-formed mountains and rugged sea coast. Rocky marine monoliths and seaweathered driftwood enhance Olympic National Park's 50 miles of Pacific Ocean beaches.

together in one gorgeous blanket of thoroughly mixed color."

The Strait of Juan de Fuca separates the park area from Canada. In 1774 the Spanish sea captain Juan Perez sailed through these waters of splendor, discovering the Olympic Mountains and originally calling them El Cerro de la Santa Rosalia. It remained for Capt. John Meares of Great Britain to explore the area in 1778 during which he named the highest peak "Mount Olympus," a designation later charted by Capt. George Vancouver.

Pacific Ocean tides break, ebb and flow against the park's western shoreline. Eastward, Puget Sound and Hood Canal form the added gift of isolation, separating, with salt water barriers, the peninsula and mainland of Washington State.

Along the fascinating shores, isolated conifers, twisted and misshapen, dot the shorelines. Then the fragmented shore, the home of the seal and wildfowl life of the sea, yields to sheer cliffs, fog-shrouded or sparkling in the sun, depending upon the day's weather. This massive moisture-channeling, aided by 142 inches of annual rainfall nourishes, on the western side, the finest remains of the Pacific Northwest rain forests.

The overwhelming impression of the rain forest is in Andrew Marvell's phrase: "a green lamp in a green shade." Or as one park service man said: "When one is inside the forest and the sun comes out, it is like being inside a giant emerald." Here, giant cone-bearing trees rise to nearly 300 feet above the forest floor. Red alders and black cottonwoods edge the stream banks where cutthroat, rainbow and brook trout thrive and steelhead seek the secluded streams in winter.

The lordly conifers dominate the realm, but here in the rain forest, the lesser fiefdoms of the tree kingdom are big-leaved and slender vine maples, burdened into arches by heavy veils of clubmoss. Most of this subsidiary civilization of the tree flourishes in openings under the dense conifer canopy. In the valleys of the Hoh, Quinault and Queets Rivers, the wondrous renewal process of future growth continues interminably as spongy, rotting undergrowth returns the nutrients to the soil where new tree life is nourished.

The disappearance of the great rain forests, which once covered a coastal area from northern California to southern Alaska, highlights the preciousness of this magnificent "remnant" in Olympic National Park. It is almost as if a splendid tropical jungle lies at the foot of the more typically Northwestern snow-covered peaks which pierce the clouds at elevations of 3,000 to 8,000 feet. Majestic Mt. Olympus dominates the uplands where more than 60 glaciers grow and recede, and these 25 square miles of ice hone down the mountains in the slow, eternal movement of time.

This mountainous interior lay unexplored until the winter of 1889-1890 when James H. Christie led the *Seattle Press* Expedition on the first crossing from Port Angeles to the Pacific Ocean. That summer, Lt. Joseph P. O'Neil led another expedition, crossing the mountains from Hood Canal to the Pacific.

Lt. O'Neil was the first to propose that the mountains would "serve admirably for a national park." A first step occurred in 1897 when President Cleveland created the Olympic Forest Reserve. A portion of the reserve was set aside as Mt. Olympus National Monument by that champion of outdoor life, President Theodore Roosevelt, in 1909. The long struggle for the permanent preservation of this vast retreat of nature ended on June 29, 1938, when Olympic National Park was established under another Roosevelt, F.D.R. Further land additions were made in 1940, 1943 and 1953, expanding the park to its authorized expanse of nearly 1,400 square miles.

The park enjoys its most favorable weather in the summer and early autumn. Although impassable snows close the higher elevations from late fall to early spring, a road is kept open, Christmas through March, from Port Angeles to the weekend ski area at Hurricane Ridge. The high-country roads and trails are usually free of snow by July.

The park's many peaks challenge both the experienced and amateur mountain climber. During June, July and August, when all 14 roads that enter the park are open, hikers and horsemen explore more than 600 miles of trails except for portions of high country where barriers of immutable snow confront the venturesome.

This is Olympic Park, a gigantic, precious gem in the diadem of America's natural beauty, stretching from coast to coast. Here, still, the conifer is supreme, symbolized by the royal Sitka spruce, with needles hard and sharp as steel, sentinel of mountain and sea, spilling the wind in a sustained whisper, or twanging its branches in the brunt of the sea blast.

Spring in Olympic is marked by the pink rhododendron, the official flower of the State of Washington.

*R*oped together for safety, mountain climbers pass craggy Blue Glacier (left) on 7,965-foot Mount Olympus, the park's highest peak. A less strenuous climb to high elevation is offered by the automobile road and nature trails at panoramic Hurricane Ridge (above left). Deep crevices ridge Blue Glacier (above), creating a spectacular setting for cross-ice pack hikes by well-equipped, seasoned climbers.

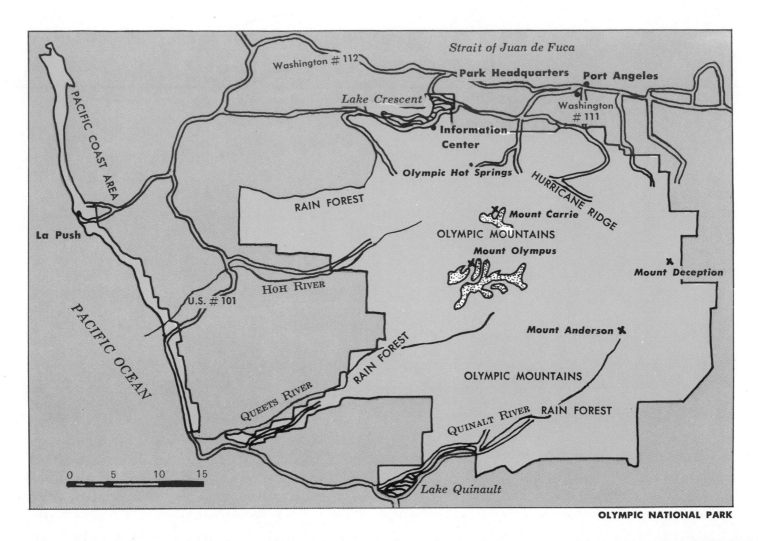

Strait of Juan de Fuca

Washington #112   Park Headquarters   Port Angeles

Lake Crescent

Information Center   Washington #111

Olympic Hot Springs   HURRICANE RIDGE

PACIFIC COAST AREA

RAIN FOREST

Mount Carrie

OLYMPIC MOUNTAINS

Mount Olympus

La Push

Mount Deception

HOH RIVER

U.S. #101

Mount Anderson

PACIFIC OCEAN

RAIN FOREST

OLYMPIC MOUNTAINS

Queets River   RAIN FOREST

QUINALT RIVER   RAIN FOREST

0 5 10 15

Lake Quinault

OLYMPIC NATIONAL PARK

Maritime fog climbs to the steep sides of snow-crowned Bailey Range (left) near the Strait of Juan de Fuca on the park's northeastern edge. At the opposite side of Olympic, the highest amount of annual rainfall in the United States creates yellow-green rain forests (above), a unique combination of towering conifers, smaller moss-covered vine maples, sword-like ferns and soft ground cover.

*M*ountain and valley vistas at Deer Park (above left) on Olympic's northeastern corner create a setting for visitor solitude. A common American wildflower, the tiger lily (right), finds an alpine home in a meadow at Hurricane Ridge. A lone deer (below) stands silhouetted amid fir trees while clouds form a fog blanket near a snow-crested mountain ridge at Olympic. The park's varied recreational fare includes a horseback climb (below left) through mountain highlands at Hayden Pass.

PETRIFIED FOREST

LOCATION: East-Central Arizona
SIZE: 94,189 acres
ESTABLISHED: 1962

Fossilized contours of an era claimed by the mists of time, and a vast horizon of alternately mingling, emerging reds, blue, browns and yellows—this is the Petrified Forest and Painted Desert combine of east-central Arizona. The "forest" of stone tree logs and trunks, coupled with the sweep of the desert's rainbow-like proscenium, constitutes a national park paradise which can be motored over, using the 34 miles of roads.

The stone forest emerges from a prehistoric period called the Triassic, over 180 million years ago, when pine-like trees grew beside streams which flowed through a seaside desert, similar to the present-day deserts of northern Chile. As best we know, the trees died of the same natural causes — fire, insects and old age — that decimate forests today. Some of the trees found in the park show signs of having been carried long distances by the early streams; others appear to have been buried where they grew.

Then the wondrous process of petrification took place along with patient sculpturing by nature. After the trees fell, they were buried by stream-carried mud and silt containing volcanic ash. In successive ages mile-thick deposits of similar material accumulated above the logs, mountain building lifted the logs far above sea level, and, comparatively recently, the logs and multicolored layers of the Painted Desert were exposed by erosion. During the time the trees were buried silica laden waters percolated into the air and pore spaces of the logs, filling these openings with multicolored quartz. Also during this period, earth tremors broke some of the logs into sections; others were fractured as erosion wore away the supporting earth.

The waters of the earth, which cyclically claim many of man's civilizations and landmarks, will, according to science, ultimately siphon away the color-charged clays, through erosion. Thus, we know that the Painted Desert will inevitably be sluiced away, as tons of silt, into the Gulf of California. Nevertheless, both the petrified logs and the wild, mixed colors of desert murals will be seen for many generations. Actually, only a part of the Petrified Forest is currently exposed. There are many other petrified logs scattered along substrata of the earth to a depth of about 300 feet.

In addition to the natural wonders preserved within the park, there exist about 300 archeological sites, spanning the period from about 300 A.D. to 1400 A.D. The pueblo (or cliff-dwelling) and other Indian cultures left in this area clear marks of their passage through time.

The unique wonder of the Painted Desert, especially for the tourist, is the titillating kaleidoscopic effect of changing colors. After rainfall, and following the shift of cloud shadows, the most stunning and varied suddenness of color combinations takes place.

Although visitors are not always conscious of the elevation of the park, it nonetheless ranges in height from 5,300 to 6,200 feet. The entire area receives less than ten inches of moisture annually and thus only hardy varieties of flowers add their smaller combina-

Brilliantly colored, the petrified logs receive their mottled patterns from oxides of iron and manganese.

tions of color to the phenomena above them.

The emphasis is upon delicate beauty with the blossoming of the yucca, mariposa-lily and cactus in the spring and the aster, painted-cup, or "paint-brush," the rabbitbrush and sunflower in bloom during the summer.

Birds, mammals, reptiles survive adequately in this barren museum of marvels. The jackrabbit, cottontail, squirrel and coyote are seen here as in other desertlands. The bobcat, porcupine and pronghorn antelope are more elusive, but omnipresent. Bird watchers know the diverse haunts of horned lark, house finch, rock wren, phoebe and sparrow in these wastes. And in this happy habitat of aridity are nearly three dozen species of snakes and lizards, including the prairie rattlesnake.

In the 1880's serious threats to the petrified wood through commercial exploitation and sheer vandalism aroused strong public protest and adroit Government action. At one point, logs were being blasted open for the amethyst crystals to be found within. Finally, on December 8, 1906, President Theodore Roosevelt created Petrified Forest National Monument by proclamation. In 1962 the area officially became Petrified Forest National Park, under the executive direction of the late President John F. Kennedy.

The park, in our own lives, and those of many future generations, exists, and will exist, for the interest and edification of the poet and beauty-lover in each of us, rather than for careless exploitation.

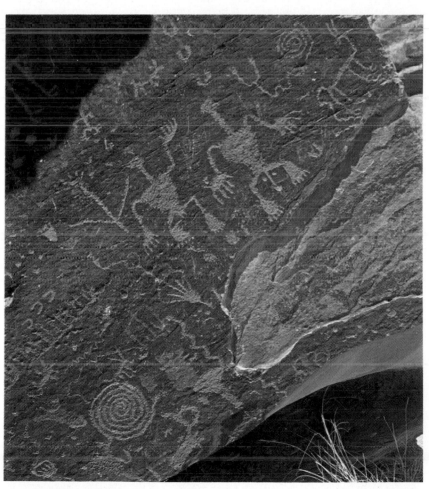

*P*ainted Desert badlands (left) are typical of badland erosion. In places a hard covering of sandstone or lava have protected the soft layers beneath from torrential summer rains to form abrupt mesas and buttes. The Painted Cliffs (top) were formed by layers of an altered volcanic ash interlayered with minute amounts of iron oxide making layers of red, blue, brown and yellow. Newspaper Rock (bottom) is a series of petroglyphs believed to depict the events in the lives of Indians there long ago.

149

A young man tries his luck in peaceful Travertine Creek, fed by two fresh-water springs that have a combined water flow of five million gallons daily.

PLATT

LOCATION: Southern Oklahoma
SIZE: 912 acres
ESTABLISHED: 1906

Peaceful Valley of Rippling Waters, the Indians called Platt National Park. The Choctaws and Chickasaws treasured its quiet groves, bubbling mineral springs astride the confluence of the western plains and the wooded hills of the east.

Platt, our smallest national park, exists because the resident Indians were rigid in conservation and generous toward their fellow Americans. They gave over their Peaceful Valley, in 1902, to the United States on condition that it be preserved for the benefit of all the people.

In 1906 this preserve which now contains 912 acres became a national park, named for Senator Orville Platt of Connecticut, who had been prominent in Indian affairs.

There are some 30 mineral and fresh water springs in the park, seeping up through three major stratas of rock. The lower, or Simpson, group of rock provides the mineral salts for the bromide and sulphur springs with their varied solutions. At the eastern end of the park fresh water courses from Buffalo and Antelope Springs, named because herds of these animals came from the surrounding prairies to drink. Today the park is a preserve for a small herd of bison.

Prairie and woodland flowers abound in the flats and glades with a proliferation of redbud trees frequently dotting this richly endowed acreage of singing waters. These surroundings provide a home for various small mammals such as raccoon and armadillo.

Platt's gift lies in the identity of understanding between Indian intuition and this brief phrase of Henry David Thoreau: "In wildness is the preservation of the world."

Stonework around Buffalo Springs (above) was constructed by the Civilian Conservation Corps during the 1930's. An aerial view (below) of Platt National Park shows its winding streams and gentle foliage.

ROCKY MOUNTAIN

LOCATION: Northern Colorado
SIZE: 259,958 acres
ESTABLISHED: 1915

High over the mile-high city of Denver, 50 miles to the northwest, is the "roof of America." The 400 or more square miles of craggy heights which we know as Rocky Mountain National Park, in the Rocky Mountains, contains 65 peaks over 10,000 feet in skyward reach.

What has been aptly called an alpine tundra is predominantly a terrain of few trees. Beyond the treeline ranges one third of the park area, with rolling, grassy slopes softening the panoramic onslaught of granite cliffs and spires.

In the two brief months of the highland summer the park is a land of enchantment, the atmosphere heady with the fragrance of tiny alpine wildflowers. In other seasons it is often bleak and desolate, windswept, with gales of arctic intensity swirling the snows into multiple hollows and crevices amid great peaks.

Far to the east, breathtakingly beautiful as seen from the uplands, the leveling edges of the Great Plains give one a literal sense of the immensity and variety of our continent. To the north, south and west, the skyline is broken by the serrated crests of other mountain ranges.

This is obviously the prime attraction for visitors: the view, as it were, from the top of our land. Unparalleled in its accessibility, because of the Trail Ridge Road, which winds through these uplands, tourists find themselves positioned, without need for the skill and strain of mountain climbing, at an elevation of 12,183 feet.

Historically, a route roughly following the Trail Ridge Road was used by the Utes and Arapahoes in crossing the Continental Divide. It was called Taieonbaa, the "Child's Trail," because it was so steep in places that children had to dismount from their horses and walk. Archeological research reveals that the Ute-Arapahoe Trail may have been in use for the past 8,000 years.

Unlike many of the Western national parks, there is little historical evidence that the area was extensively used by either Indians or whites in the exploration and winning of the West. Hunting parties from the tribes on either side of the Divide visited the area in summer on hunting trips. Berry-picking and just plain recreation were not unknown in these calming haunts. Trappers assessed the fur-bearing potential of the region — these, the informal explorers, must have been familiar with Longs Peak, awesomely viewed from the plains below. Two more formal parties, Lt. Zebulon Pike in 1806, and Major Stephen H. Long in 1820 — for whom the peak was named—charted the uncharted for future generations.

Hallett Peak in the Bear Lake area is one of 107 named peaks over 11,000 feet above sea level in the park.

In 1859 Joel Estes discovered the valley which was to bear his name. He moved his family to the "gorgeous gorge" and thus initiated further settlement of the town and valley now familiar as Estes Park.

The tremendous potential of the expanse of glaciated landscapes, as a national park, was grasped and articulated by surveyor and conservationist Enos Mills. At the tender age of 16 he had built a home in the Longs Peak valley in 1886. In 1891 he had filled his spirit enduringly working with a survey party in the Yellowstone. With a ferocity born of dedication to, and belief in conservation, he fought unceasingly for the ultimate establishment of Rocky Mountain National Park in 1915. Mills died in 1922, but some of his statements seem to have a touch of the immortality of the Rockies he loved and fought for: "Room — glorious room," he wrote, "room in which to find ourselves."

Today, about two million visitors annually enjoy the rugged and untrammeled beauty of the area. Meadows resplendent with wildflowers; forests of pine, spruce and fir; a variety of wild creatures in their natural habitat: American elk (wapiti), mule deer, black bear, coyote, cougar, can be glimpsed throughout lower and higher ranges of the park.

The solemn and symbolic bighorn, largest of American wild sheep, can be sighted — sandy-brown in summer, grayish-brown in winter — at Sheep Lake and on lonely promontories near Milner Pass in the northwest section of the park. The methodical beaver, lord of his dams, can be observed at several locations, including Horseshoe Park or Moraine Park, near the visitor center. In immaculate, pebble-bottomed streams, astringent with shallow, crystalline waters, stingingly frigid, fish trend toward anglers awaiting them in the lower levels. Trout is the resident of Rocky Mountain waters: brook, rainbow, cutthroat, with the latter native to the area. One of the principal lakes is Bear Lake in the south-central section.

Winter programs, the ski run and the ski lodge, are active around Hidden Valley, eight miles west of park headquarters. But springtime is the season of the Rockies, the season of bright wildflowers on the sunny slopes; and the meadows are a painter's heaven. Snow flurries with the sun's decline but does not endure before the heavy glare of the noonday sun. Summer in the park's tundra region doesn't really begin until July, but it is always summer in the spirit when the peace of the mountain grandeur descends upon those who seek its benisons.

154

From the Trail Ridge Road, the visitor can see from his car such sights as the Mummy Range (above).
The road is often above the timberline (overleaf) where one can stop to view unusual rock formations.

With myriad lakes in rustic settings (above), one of the recreational offerings of Rocky Mountain is fishing. Fish in the park include cutthroat, brook, brown and rainbow trout. Rocky Mountain is the home of the bighorn sheep (above right), the wild sheep of the mountains. Known for speed, agility and endurance, this sheep, with massive, tightly curled horns, lives in mountains high above the timberline.

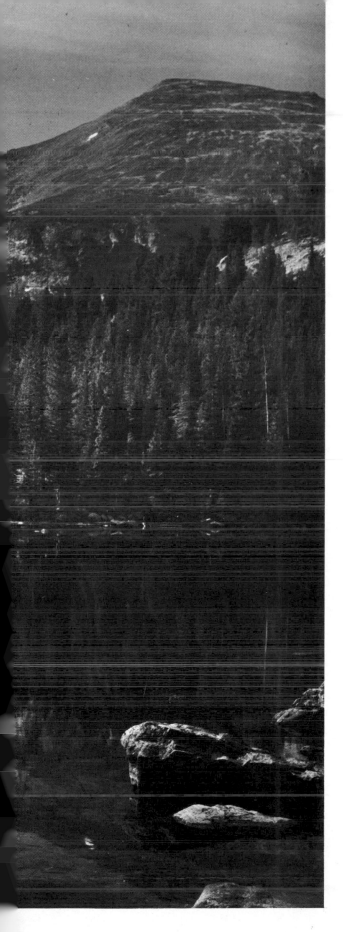

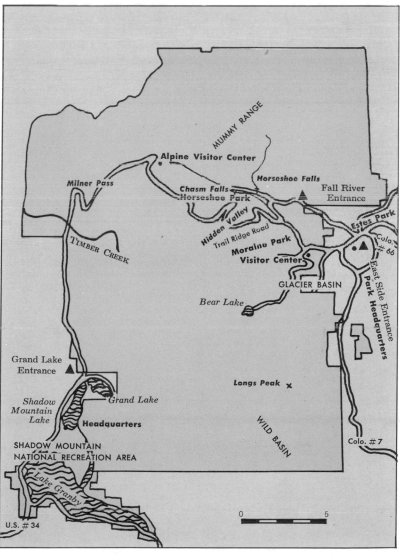

ROCKY MOUNTAIN NATIONAL PARK

Old in appearance, the Sierras in Sequoia are geologically young. Autumn colors cottonwoods below Mt. Langely (above), 14,042 feet high. On horse, a rider (right) enjoys Evolution Valley in Kings Canyon.

SEQUOIA

LOCATION: Southeast-Central California
SIZE: 385,413 acres
ESTABLISHED: 1890

and
KINGS CANYON

LOCATION: Southeast-Central California
SIZE: 459,306 acres
ESTABLISHED: 1940

The tree is king here, peering down over a majestic domain of gray granite mountains, deep forests and valleys making a harsh but welcoming slash in the landscape. It stands, holding silent court over a seemingly untouched panorama, beginning beyond one horizon and going past the other.

This tree is the largest living thing in the world — rivaling the age of any tree or other plant known — the sequoia, gently elbowing aside white firs and sugar pines, its cinnamon-red bark and pointed needles quite unchanged from the time when frightening creatures rumbled the earth with their ponderous tread.

One can count nearly 4,000 years since some of them were born, and science believes none has died simply because of old age. They usually find their life-giving roots exposed by slow erosion, perhaps nature's way to return organic material to the soil. Then they topple and die with a crash, to lie fallen beside other warriors fighting the long battle against time in Sequoia and Kings Canyon National Parks.

There are more than 1,300 square miles in the two parks, starting at the foothills of the San Joaquin Valley and reaching toward the crest of the High Sierra. It is some 6,000 feet above sea level here, and the altitude makes the giant sequoias seem all the more regal. Perhaps at first, the height leaves one breathless, then suddenly the vista generates a catch in the lungs, for nowhere else does such a view exist.

Save for the efforts of a few, these mighty trees might have disappeared to the logger. The basis of the two parks gained Federal protection in 1890 so that they could be preserved. The culmination of this protection came in 1940 with the establishment of Kings Canyon National Park.

Hale Tharp was the first recorded visitor, a brawny, tanned cattleman seeking grazing land. He went up the Kaweah Valley near what is now Moro Rock, and listened to an Indian friend tell of the great mountain meadows lying beyond. Heartened, for cattle were his livelihood, Tharp followed the patrol of Indians to the meadows carpeted with deep, nutritional grass. There, in 1858, he beheld the Giant Forest's sequoias, and set up a temporary home in a fallen tree hollowed by fire.

Then, in 1862, Joseph Thomas discovered the General Grant Grove (now located in Kings Canyon Park) where several of the parks' outstanding trees reign. It took little time for their descriptions, and those of others, to create a national stir to preserve this virgin land.

Today, it all has changed. The parks are not what they were a century ago, nor are the trees the same. Although most of the changes are too small to measure, the valleys *are* a bit deeper because of erosion, the mountains a shade lower because of the torture of the elements, and some trees taller because the protective ring of the Government has given them life. If anything, Sequoia and Kings Canyon have grown more graceful, bearing their years with dignity.

The nucleus of a visit here is the General Sherman Tree, largest of all living things on earth, towering more than 272 feet above the ground and measuring more than 35 feet across the base. Because it is hard to imagine such a tree, perhaps this helps: the trunk alone weighs approximately 1,450 tons and has 50,010 cubic feet of wood, enough to build about 40 homes. The General Grant is only five feet shorter and contains only a bit less wood.

These giants of the forest live in harmony with their smaller and shorter-lived brethren. The gigantic sugar pines and firs wrest life from the soil, and even without the sequoias their existence would be a pleasing sight. They are youngsters, however, for the General Sherman is believed to be more than 3,500 years old, a fertile tree when Christ was born and existing when the great pyramids of ancient Egypt were being built. It is a living link with history; no, more than history, the evolution of our planet. Only one existing thing has been proved older, the bristlecone pine. And the young sequoias may be living after our civilization has become history.

Smaller than the sequoias, but with much value of their own, are the flora and fauna of the two parks. The floor of the forest is covered with dogwood, colorful lupine and the red-flowered snow plant. Meadows are filled with wildflowers, Sierra shooting stars in June, Queen Anne's lace and Senecio later. Bear and mule deer roam at will.

This is a rugged land, existing almost as a separate entity from the rest of the West. Beyond the Giant Forest, named by that great, Scots-born naturalist, John Muir, is the Sierra Nevada's high country, a vast, tilted block on the earth where snow-capped peaks — crowned by Mount Whitney, the highest mountain in the United States outside of Alaska —

The biggest and among the oldest of living things is the sequoia tree, sequoia gigantea.

vast, tilted block on the earth where snow-capped peaks — crowned by Mount Whitney, the highest mountain in the United States outside of Alaska — rise to more than 14,000 feet to cast giant shadows on glacial valleys and ice-formed lake basins. This landscape is relatively untouched, existing as it is by Federal decree.

Here the bighorn sheep forages and the wolverine hunts among the alpine solitude, nuzzling through the luxuriant growth of a short summer, growing fat before the chill winds blow away the fragrance of delicate flowers and turn their vivid shades to dull brown, their colors not to return until spring.

Great canyons are incised upon the landscape, among the deepest to be found in the United States. Gorges along the middle and south forks of the Kings River are more than a mile deep, their steep sides forming a canyon between the great peaks and the roaring waters tumbling over time-polished stones below.

Here there are valleys, miles long and a half-mile wide, created when small streams grew larger and carried infinitesimal bits of stone with their downhill fury, then finally hewn to shape by vast fields of ice jamming their depths. The valleys bear silent testament to their past; glacial moraines telling of when nature's strength rubbed, scoured and finally gouged

its way through granite, forming the canyon walls we see today.

Some of these valleys are covered with forests of ponderosa pine, incense-cedar and white fir, towering above blue lupine waving in the summer breeze. Deer, bear and bobcats graze and hunt among the trees. Birds flutter against wind gusts, then swoop earthward to grasp an insect in their beaks and retreat to the forest a few wing flaps beyond to enjoy their meal and perhaps sing of triumph.

High above — nearly two miles on top of the level of the sea — is a mountain wilderness dotted with glacial lakes mirroring the sun and its spectacular surroundings.

Magnificent, even in winter when snow festoons the giant sequoias and fills the dips and small valleys, there is no word that does justice to the parks and their environs.

The region so moved John Muir that he wrote, "No doubt these trees would make good lumber after passing through a saw mill, as George Washington after passing through the hands of a French chef would have made good food."

The sequoias, thankfully, are living, for their peculiar makeup gives them an odds-on chance against every natural enemy — except perhaps man.

While living in a cabin built in a single, fallen sequoia tree (left), Hale D. Tharp, the first white man to see the Giant Forest, used the area as a summer range for 30 years. The mule deer (above) finds a natural habitat at Sequoia with its forests, rocky uplands and brushy areas. Although the General Grant Tree (right) is the second largest of all sequoias, it is still 100 feet higher than Niagara Falls. This tree now serves as a shrine to America's war dead.

Nestled among decaying litter of pine and fir needles is the snow plant, a bright saprophyte.

Giants in the fog, the sequoias, have lived 40 centuries, protected by two-foot thick bark.

The flowering deer brush, or New Jersey tea, is a brilliant foreground to glacier-polished peaks of the Sierra Nevada. Favoring dry woodlands and high areas, it is a good winter food for grazing stock.

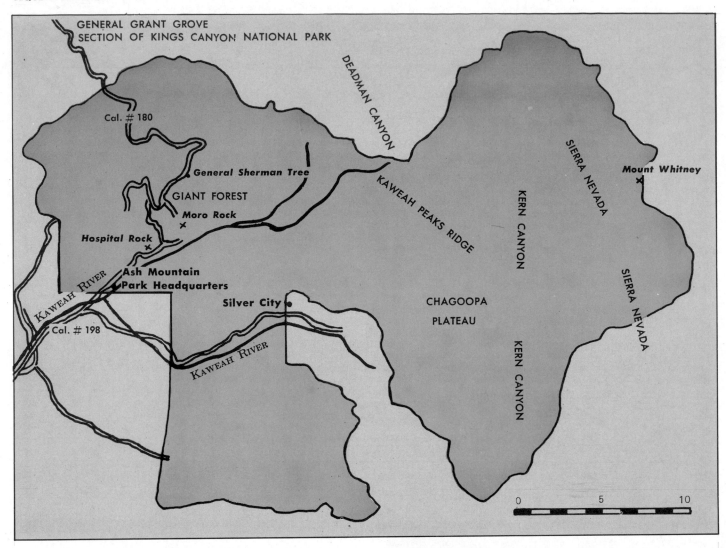

Map labels:
GENERAL GRANT GROVE SECTION OF KINGS CANYON NATIONAL PARK
DEADMAN CANYON
SIERRA NEVADA
Cal. # 180
Mount Whitney
General Sherman Tree
GIANT FOREST
Moro Rock
KAWEAH PEAKS RIDGE
KERN CANYON
Hospital Rock
Ash Mountain Park Headquarters
KAWEAH RIVER
Silver City
CHAGOOPA PLATEAU
Cal. # 198
KAWEAH RIVER
SIERRA NEVADA
KERN CANYON
0   5   10

Kearsarge Pass (right), at Kings Canyon, is over 11,500 feet above sea level. From there, mountain climbers can see rugged pinnacles of the same name. Tunnel Rock (above right), a man-made phenomena on the General's Highway, a half-mile from Sequoia's Ash Mountain Entrance Station, requires a by-pass road for many because of low clearance. Sparseness of trees at Pinchot Pass (far right), at over 12,000 feet, testifies that the pass is near the timberline.

168

The frequent bluish haze (above), for which Blue Ridge Parkway was named, is evident at Craggy Gardens near Asheville. Symbol of days past is the Brinegar Cabin (right) where historic looms are still used.

SHENANDOAH

LOCATION: Northwestern Virginia
SIZE: 193,646 acres
ESTABLISHED: 1935

and

BLUE RIDGE PARKWAY

LOCATION: Virginia and North Carolina
LENGTH: 469 miles
ESTABLISHED: 1936

This is a humble place where beauty is quiet and does not shout, where there is a tranquillity, a charm of blushing shyness that only gradually captures the visitor's awareness. But once its cup of gentle refreshment is drunk, one will find his pleasure and more.

This is Shenandoah, cradled against the breast of gentle mountains grown mellow with the age of the eastern half of our continent, spread in a generous north-south sweep down northwestern Virginia, encompassing great but not unconquerable mountains and brooks running in a grandfatherly way through the coolness of stately trees.

Yet, compared with other national parks, Shenandoah seems a lesser light until first the geological history is realized; finally its subtlety shines and one realizes there are few places left that can match its serenity. "Oh, Shenandoah, I Love Your Daughter," pleads the American folk song, and one wonders if its composer refers to the daughter of an Indian chief or the land named for the sachem. It is moot, for Shenandoah whispers of love, love of the land and its creatures.

This scene of green coolness and a long mountain range like a vein of blue is a great gift, for within a day's drive, over half of the nation's population can escape the tedium and anxieties of urban existence and sink into its quiet pleasure.

The Blue Ridge Mountains were first seen by Captain John Smith, and later by Alexander Spotswood, the Colonial governor of Virginia who crossed near what is now Swift Run Gap. George Freeman Pollock visited the Blue Ridge in 1886, and inspired by its beauty, spent a lifetime building a resort on Stony Man Mountain to let others succumb to the region's charm.

Pollock and friends proposed Shenandoah to a national committee, formed in 1925 to seek suitable park sites in the East. It was not an easy time for them; they struggled most of a night answering the committee's questionnaire, finishing it only a scant few hours ahead of the deadline.

Harry Flood Byrd, Sr., then governor of Virginia, supported their proposal and appointed his commissioner of conservation and development to oversee the purchase of lands for Shenandoah. The state legislature appropriated a million dollars, a vast sum in that time of hard cash, to help the park along. Added to it was a $1¼ million in the pennies, nickels and dimes of Virginians and others.

It was not until the eve of the Fourth of July, 1936, that Shenandoah National Park was a reality. President Franklin Delano Roosevelt dedicated it in ceremonies at Big Meadows, for the "recreation and re-creation which we shall find here."

Re-creation. It is two things spelled one way; only the pronunciation is different. For many who see Shenandoah, the accent is on the first syllable, for they are re-created here. They usually come by the Skyline Drive, a winding, 105-mile road threading across the crest of the Blue Ridge, offering 75 parking overlooks of the valleys and mountain slopes. Often they stop to leave the pavement and walk some of the 200 miles of foot trails. The hardy few who traverse the entire Appalachian Trail walk through Shenandoah, more than 90 miles of it.

Walking is the best way to enjoy the subtle pleasures of the park, such as seeing water shift its course to the other side of a rock, or feeling beneath one's feet the crunch of the brown, needle-strewn floor of the forest. A few yards beyond may be a handful of gnarled apple trees, unpruned for generations, surrounding a small clearing being rapidly overgrown with trees. Look closely, for here was the cabin of an early settler, one of the fur-capped frontiersmen who crossed these mountains on their way west. Some continued on, some remained. These old mountains were not really much of a natural barrier, but one so attractive many stayed, making it their home.

Hikers often climb Old Rag Mountain, starting near Nethers, Virginia, to complete the ascent and descent of eight miles in a day. There are shelters nearby. Others clop slowly along on horseback on the miles of bridle paths lacing the park.

The Shenandoah Valley was recognized as the Confederacy's "bread basket" and the back door to the nation's capital during the Civil War. General Stonewall Jackson brought troops within the park's boundaries during the struggle, and in Browns Gap there are earthworks believed to have been built by Confederate forces when they occupied the pass.

This is an old part of our land; more than a billion years in creation. Craggy peaks were smoothed by time into the gentle slopes of today, often wearing a mantle of the blue haze which gave the famous Blue Ridge its name.

The four seasons are each brilliant, painting new colors on the landscape from a palette of pastels with a handful of vivid shades. The dogwood and redbud come early in the spring as leaves from the 80-odd species of trees begin to unfold in the new-found warmth. Nearly seven-eighths of the park is forested, and in deep shaded glades the winter snows disappear slowly. Finally the sun brushes away the last patches of white, the water seeping into the ground to give life to plant and animal alike, often appearing as a cool spring a mile away or cascading down a rill.

Then the azaleas and locust come into bloom, followed by the pink and white mountain laurel. In patches of deep shade live the Dutchman's Breeches, a delicate, odd-appearing wildflower sharing the rich, moist soil with beard tongue and red blossoms of the cardinal-flower. Pushing its way through the carpet of black leaves here and there is the snowy trillium, a cousin of the turk's-cap lily covering low, grassy meadows.

In fall, as summer gives way to a new season, so that living things might sleep and regain their strength for a new spring, so that the mountain laurel will bloom again—come the colors, the wild reds, oranges, yellows and browns.

The Blue Ridge Parkway, separately administered but actually an extension of Shenandoah and Great Smokies National Parks, winds slowly from its lowest elevation crossing the James River in Virginia upward to its highest point of more than 6,000 feet in elevation in the Balsams south of Asheville, North Carolina. From it one can see the rolling hills of the Virginia Piedmont, across the fertile fields of the Great Valley, to the Alleghenies and then onward to the Black Mountains and the Great Smokies. Adjacent to the parkway are three national forests — the George Washington, the Jefferson and the Pisgah, which contains the first large tract of managed forest in this country.

In North Carolina's Black Mountains, Mt. Mitchell, 6,684 feet above sea level, is the highest peak in the eastern United States. Like other summits in the Blacks and the high Balsams, it is covered with spruce and fir, the two species of evergreens common to the wilds of Canada. Deer, bear, squirrels and one of the two herds of elk east of the Rockies roam up and down the mountainsides.

The parkway area is also rich in the folk history of the late 1700's: Log cabins and gristmills are preserved; Daniel Boone's Wilderness Road crosses the parkway in North Carolina.

Pleasures on a human scale are abundant in Shenandoah or along the Blue Ridge Parkway.

With much of Shenandoah forested, the 75 parking overlooks give excellent panoramas of the scenic hillsides.

As the Blue Ridge Parkway extends 469 miles through the Southern Appalachian Mountains, it tells the story of the original settlers, independent mountain people, through their homesteads and settlements.

Autumn is beautiful at Shenandoah and the Blue Ridge Parkway for then the trees catch fire with color.

A bird of the forests, the wild turkey finds a good life in the thickly wooded mountains of Shenandoah.

Marby Mill was built in the late 1700's when Blue Ridge marked the edge of the western frontier. In use until 1936, it is preserved today with several other structures as evidence of a pioneer past.

SHENANDOAH NATIONAL PARK

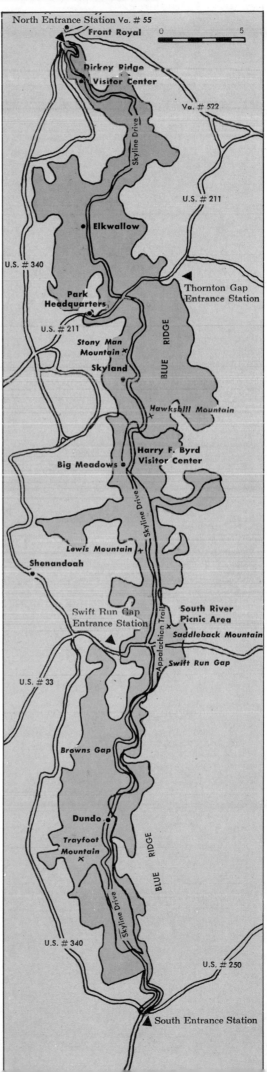

North Entrance Station Va. # 55
Front Royal

Dickey Ridge
Visitor Center

Skyline Drive

Va. # 522

U.S. # 211

Elkwallow

U.S. # 340

Thornton Gap
Entrance Station

Park
Headquarters

BLUE RIDGE

U.S. # 211

Stony Man
Mountain ×

Skyland

Hawksbill Mountain ×

Harry F. Byrd
Visitor Center

Big Meadows ●

Skyline Drive

Lewis Mountain +

Shenandoah

Appalachian Trail

Swift Run Gap
Entrance Station

South River
Picnic Area

× Saddleback Mountain

Swift Run Gap

U.S. # 33

Browns Gap

Dundo ●

Trayfoot
Mountain ×

BLUE RIDGE

Skyline Drive

U.S. # 340

U.S. # 250

South Entrance Station

VIRGIN ISLANDS

LOCATION: Virgin Islands (St. John Island)
SIZE: 11,031 acres
ESTABLISHED: 1956

The essence of the Caribbean's soft, luxuriant, provocative moods is nowhere better captured than at Trunk Bay of Virgin Islands National Park. The green waters are rich with multihued varieties of colorful coral, sponges and exotic tropical fish. The shimmering white beaches are fringed with palms. Off shore stands an occasional islet. Above, a royal blue sky. Inland, the dominant terrain is composed of rugged tropical forests and Bordeaux Mountain, 1,277 feet high.

The park constitutes two-thirds of the Island of St. John, which is nine miles in length. The islands form a geological unit with Puerto Rico and the Greater Antilles, being of volcanic origin. St. John Island is a typical offspring of subsurface volcanic eruptions, dating back millions of years. Steep mountains, deep valleys, gleaming white beaches and extensive coral reefs growing on an underwater shelf of rock are characteristic of this unique national preserve. These are the islands that were discovered by Christopher Columbus on his second voyage, in 1493. He named them in honor of St. Ursula and her 11,000 virgins.

Prior to the incursions of the Europeans, villages of the peaceful Arawak Indians dotted the shores of St. John. Rock carvings called petroglyphs can still be seen here, suggestive of ancient shrines. Prepared to give Columbus and his succeeding voyagers a warm reception, however, were the fierce Caribs who had come from South America a century earlier and were encroaching steadily on Arawak lands.

After 1493, Dutch, English, Spanish, French and Danish explorers came to the Virgin Islands. The Danes, who left a more permanent mark, did not establish themselves on St. John until 1717. Arable land was cultivated for sugar and cotton crops and the plantations were manned by slaves imported from Africa. The sugar trade flourished until slavery was abolished in 1848, an economic and social blow to a powerful planter aristocracy. The ex-slaves turned to fishing, charcoalmaking, cattle raising, but they and their picturesque descendants remained generally poor. Tourism is currently the primary industry of the islands.

Following the demise of the plantations in the mid-1800's, tropical forests inexorably returned substantial areas of the island to its "natural habitat." Thus, the island resembles the one which Columbus first looked upon, plus the exotic flowers, trees and shrubs introduced by the settlers. Amid tropical luxuriance, however, the ruins of Danish sugar mills can still be seen.

Strategically commanding approaches to the Caribbean and Atlantic as they do, the islands were of great interest to the security of the United States. Thus, intensive negotiations, at first unsuccessful, took place

Dating from the mid-1700's, the Annaberg estate ruins emerge from a green promontory above Leinster Bay.

between the American Government and Denmark, beginning in 1867. The islands were finally purchased in 1917 for $25 million, administered earlier by the U.S. Navy, and later by a resident Governor.

The relatively moist interior highlands of St. John, including steep-walled valleys, are dominated by a jungle forest of evergreen hardwoods. Drier slopes contain broad-leaved trees. Mangroves, turpentines, maho, cinnamon-bay kapok and soursop are the characteristic trees. Flowering shrubs and trees bloom in season, with a charm for the tourists increased by the knowledge that hibiscus, flamboyant, frangipani, bougainvillea, are expensive commercial items back in the floral hothouses of the States.

About 100 species of birds abound in the islands with land birds more dominant. Herons, egrets, pelicans, gulls, frigate birds and terns can, however, be spotted along the shores. The pearly-eyed thrasher, smooth-billed ani, the mocking and humming birds are discernible in the forests and hills.

Six forms of bats are the only native mammals, although several species have been introduced, the best known being the mongoose. There are also toads, lizards, turtles, snakes and the hermit crab, which, oddly, lives in discarded top shells. Insects are minimal with the exception of the mosquito and pesky sand fly which multiply after rainy spells.

Snorkeling is a major activity in the park. Visitors have a chance to snorkel along the underwater trail at Trunk Bay, participate in a naturalist-led snorkel trip at Turtle or Cinnamon Bays or explore on their own in a number of other good snorkeling areas (Hawksnest, Leinster, Francis and Lameshur Bays). The water here is warm and clear. The commonly seen features of this marine world are antler, brain and star corals (that make up the reef's structure); gorgonians (sea fans, sea plumes and sea whips); sponges; and a great variety of colorful marine fishes.

The northeast trade winds temper the intense heat of the tropical sun, yielding pleasantly warm days and cool nights. The average annual temperature is 79 degrees with only about 6 degrees difference between the winter and summer seasons. The lowest temperature on record is 60 degrees, the highest, 96. It is readily apparent why winter is the busiest visitors' season.

St. John Island's beauty, spiced with coral reef, tropical forest and history, is a matchless part of the national heritage.

Caneel Bay (above), site of the park's most extensive guest facilities, is also an excellent area for sailing. Bayside cottages and beach units for visitors now stand where European plantation owners grew cotton and sugar cane in the 18th century. Expert gliders, ring-billed gulls (above right) fly gracefully near the multihued sea and lush green woodlands. Trunk Bay (right) features a self-guiding underwater trail through spectacular natural displays of coral and other marine life for experienced snorkel swimmers.

*J*ungle forests (left) dominate the interior highlands and ravines of the park, their rapid growth requiring constant clearing by machete-wielding trail workers. The sugar mill ruins at Annaberg (above), are among several stone reminders of St. John Island's history. Built by European settlers who established large plantations in the early 1700's, the structures became fortifications during a slave uprising in 1733.

WIND CAVE

LOCATION: Southwestern South Dakota
SIZE: 28,059 acres
ESTABLISHED: 1903

Wind Cave's 44 square miles above ground contain many bison, as well as deer, elk and other wildlife.

The wind blows east, the wind blows west, and from the other two points of the compass, also. But it doesn't usually blow up through the ground. Yet cowboy Tom Bingham, wandering through the southern Black Hills in 1881, felt the upward draft and stooped in puzzlement, touched with wonder. There he saw a ten-inch natural opening in the limestone rock of the hill — and what could he call it but Wind Cave.

Afterward, explorers got into the cave by digging entrances near the original "blow-hole." Within were the fairyland formations on walls and ceilings, resembling a honeycomb or "boxwork" structure that might have intrigued a Tom Sawyer and Huck Finn into dark and forbidding recesses.

One might first imagine that another aperture higher on the hill would be the air intake. But that is not the case. This strange phenomenon of a breathing hill is believed to be caused by changes in atmospheric pressure. The cave actually completes the cycle of breathing, as it were, by letting in the wind when the outside pressure rises, and by expelling air when the pressure drops.

The weird ornamentation of Wind Cave is unique among famed caverns in that it includes relatively few stalagmites and stalactites. The boxwork was created by a layer of limestone which was sculptured and form-frozen in varied periods of geological uplift and submergence. Then, moisture containing calcium carbonate, seeped through and evaporated, depositing the calcium carbonate, forming calcite in the cracks.

More recently the limestone between the fissures dissolved, leaving calcite fins, some lace-like, some broad enough to resemble the sides of boxes and thus called "boxwork." This variegated effulgence is additionally decorated with arresting displays of mineral colors in the form of tiny, sparkling crystals called "frostwork" and formations that look like yuletide arrangements of "popcorn."

The central attraction of Wind Cave National Park, the cavern, is rivaled in naturalistic lure by the wildlife sanctuary surrounding it. Over the park's 44 square miles of rolling woodlands and plains, graze herds of the historic bison, once slaughtered by callous white men from Pullman car and saddle alike. The bison, more popularly known as buffalo, is rich in legend. Staff of life for the Indians, and the shield against wind and storm in the hides of the red men's teepees, the bison later became a thoroughly American symbol in terms of the settlement of the wild West. Antelope, elk and deer, in herds, also graze among the lush rises and flatlands of the park.

Biologically speaking, east meets west in Wind Cave National Park, where ponderosa pine, typical of the Western mountains, grow on the same slopes with eastern bur oaks. And the animals graze on what is a prime example of mixed-grass prairie, a rich natural blending of medium tall and short grasses, with a sprinkling of wildflowers which lend dashes of color to the scene.

Here, in virginal splendor, is one of the last of the portions of the great Western plains. Here in South Dakota are wonders in number: the breathing cave; the historic, wild sea of grass, rippling in the wind; the mighty buffalo.

*P*ark ranger (left) viewing park's landscape. "Chandelier boxwork" in Temple Room (above) is fine example of the unique formation for which Wind Cave is known. Pasqueflower (top right) is South Dakota's state flower. Pronghorn (bottom right), one of the two sole living American kinds of antelope, makes its home in the park.

YELLOWSTONE

LOCATION: Northwestern Wyoming, Eastern Idaho and
Southern Montana

SIZE: 2,213,207 acres

ESTABLISHED: 1872

It is like the creation of the very devil himself: Angry forces of the underworld locked in combat beneath the earth with the sounds and visible fury of their struggle seeping through fissures to enthrall the curious above ground who come to see what the forces of fire and ice have spawned.

This is Yellowstone National Park in the northwest corner of Wyoming (and narrow strips of Idaho and Montana), where nearly all that nature has to offer has been concentrated in a spectacular display unmatched anywhere on earth. Boiling springs, steam vents, mudpots spewing mud and, as a climax, the great geysers hurtling tons of water hundreds of feet skyward — these dot the otherwise pastoral land to make a strangely beautiful if not sometimes forbidding world.

The park's strange landscape had its origin some 20 million years ago when Yellowstone, then a mountain-rimmed basin, became the seat of violent volcanism. Clouds of dust and ash filled the air. Settling shroud-like over the land, it buried entire forests. Fiery cascades of semi-molten rock rolled down the mountainsides, and great fissures belched forth enormous volumes of highly fluid lava. Some 600 cubic miles of this molten rock was spewed out onto the land. The mountain-rimmed basin filled; it was a basin no longer, and Yellowstone became a high plateau.

But a few scars remained, as did a handful of open wounds which could never quite heal because of the cancerous fury far beneath. The heat of these prehistoric volcanoes remains, much like a storage battery to provide power for the sights which greet the visitor today.

Old Faithful is aptly named, for it is prompt, appearing about once an hour, day and night, hurling 15,000 gallons of hot water in a single, magnificent unleashing of force. There are few other places in the world where such phenomena exist — New Zealand, Chile and Iceland.

Old Faithful has 200 cousins at Yellowstone, among them the Riverside, Grotto, Castle and Beehive geysers, all sustained in the same way. Cold water from the long winter's melted snows finds its way through the hard volcanic rock around the geysers. Thousands of feet below the surface it is heated by hot rocks and also by gases and natural steam escaping from still deeper molten rock. Soon the cool water begins to boil, building pressure as steam forms, forcing the water higher into the geyser column. Then as the pressure is relaxed, huge quantities of steam are formed within the underground chambers, forcing the column of water to the surface in a pulsating, continuous finger of dancing liquid, pirouetting on the surface for four or five minutes. Suddenly the mad ballet ends, the crown of vapor floats skyward and the water recedes as the energy of the steam dissipates. Then, it begins again in the mighty flexing of muscles which has become America's best-known natural wonder.

With this fire which has shaped the face of Yellowstone, there is also ice — the great glaciers which formed on the mountains to the north and east when the fires cooled and died, on the surface at least. These unyielding masses, some 1,000 and more feet thick, began to move downward, bringing with them the inorganic scrapings of the land over which they passed. Small valleys were deepened and widened,

Sunlight captures the power of steaming water as it erupts from Castle Geyser at Yellowstone National Park.

some mountains were sharpened and others ground level. The ice melted, leaving lakes which have long since disappeared.

The rest of Yellowstone is not quite so forbidding, but has a rugged loveliness all its own: A cliff of obsidian, or black volcanic glass, overlooks columns of lava rock; a steady flow of the hot springs is seen a few miles beyond Obsidian Cliff; fossil forests exist in silence not too far from craggy mountains caressed with the green of conifers; a multitude of wildlife roams fearlessly through great forests of pine; roaring waterfalls plummet into a yellow rock canyon, the sun forming a rainbow above its splashing waters.

The stories of the early travelers to Yellowstone, such as John Colter in 1807-1808, were looked upon with skepticism. But the tales continued, and finally in 1870 Yellowstone was officially "discovered." Two years later it became the nation's and the world's first national park.

Even after it became the first of the great park system, it was not a safe place for tourists. While some Indians possibly lived in fear of the geysers, the Bannocks, Shoshones, Blackfeet and Crows raided and murdered hunters, trappers and explorers. In 1877, the Nez Perce turned to violence, killing some visitors, then burned a ranch north of the park.

Yellowstone's noises of the 20th century are not those of war-painted red men, but those of winds brushing tree limbs, the rumble of water crashing to far-below canyons and the whisper of rain on the high plateau. It is the sound of deer and American elk (wapiti) browsing on the deep green carpet of meadows, the rattle of stones under the feet of the majestic bighorn sheep clambering up a steep wash, the frightened snort of the pronghorn antelope fleeing into the wind, the earth-shaking rumble of the great and shaggy buffalo racing red-eyed across a flat plain, the mournful cry of the coyote and the angry roar of the grizzly bear.

These creatures, one of the greatest concentrations of native American wildlife in the nation, roam about the park in impressive numbers, joining to drink in spring and fall at the pools where great flights of migrating waterfowl pause to rest. They each have found their environmental niche at Yellowstone, wading in the marshes, flitting from tree to tree or browsing on tender green shoots in the forests where there is a cool respite from the summer sun.

High above much of the park is Yellowstone Lake, a body of water stretching 20 miles in one direction, 14 in the other. Its mirror-like surface can be broken into giant whitecaps within minutes as storms blow in from the snow-capped Rockies beyond, or great bolts of lightning are discharged between the surface and the sky.

Travel this lake in a boat to its outlet where the Yellowstone River begins its course, a clear, swift-running stream knifing through green forests and past grassy meadows. Then the soft but persistent stream becomes more determined as it shoots out in a straight line to the base of the Upper Falls 109 feet below. A deep gorge holds it fast until the burgeoning water pours over the lip of the Lower Falls through a narrow notch, dropping more than 300 feet accompanied by a thunderous crash and gale of wind. It is here, where the river has cut over a thousand feet into the highly colored rocks, that the Grand Canyon of the Yellowstone begins. This, one of the most beautiful of canyons in the world, is best viewed from Artist's Point, Inspiration Point or Grandview.

The weather, like the park itself, has great contrasts. Winters are fierce and snow falls relentlessly to fill great earth cavities. Storms make cruel blows at the plateaus, bringing awesome amounts of snow and ice. It melts slowly, but fortunately it arrives each year, for without this ponderous volume of water the geysers would fail, the hot springs dwindle to a trickle then die and finally the two spectacular falls would become but a dribble and streams would dry, upsetting the ecological balance of all that lies to the south.

But fortunately, it seems nothing will change in Yellowstone for the forces of nature are not easily swayed. Here there is no man-made edifice or unnatural changes by machine. There is no skyscraper, except some of rock, or hole torn in the earth, except the slowly evolving depression caused by water and wind today and the volcanoes or glaciers of yesterday. There is peace and ultimate grandeur in Yellowstone, a legacy left by nature and administered for all the heirs of tomorrow.

The Absaroka Mountains extend for 175 miles into northwestern Wyoming including Yellowstone National Park.

*G*rizzly bears (right), which enjoy the refuge of Yellowstone, are the largest and most to be feared of the bear family. These massive bears do not climb trees but can scramble about the roughest mountains with dexterity. Park visitors are forbidden to feed the grizzly which rarely hibernates and is an attraction all year round. At the southwest corner of the park is Cave Falls (below right), one of the hundreds of spots that attract photographers, both professional and tourist. Fishing Bridge (below) spans the Yellowstone River at its mouth as fishermen try for rainbow, lake and black spotted trout.

Canoeists on Yellowstone Lake have a mighty backdrop with the Absaroka Mountains to the east.

A gnarled ponderosa pine looks on the Grand Canyon of the Yellowstone from the top of Mount Washburn.

Calcium carbonate deposits terrace colorfully at Mammoth Hot Springs forming a quasi-frozen waterfall.

The Lower Falls of Yellowstone River (above) changes 1,200 cubic feet of bottlegreen water into frothy white jets plunging 309 feet into the gorge below.

Old Faithful Geyser (below) erupts regularly every 65 minutes shooting 15,000 gallons of water 125-175 feet into the air. Eruptions last several minutes.

Early evening skies are reflected in the Firehole River as it meanders past the Midway Geyser Basin.

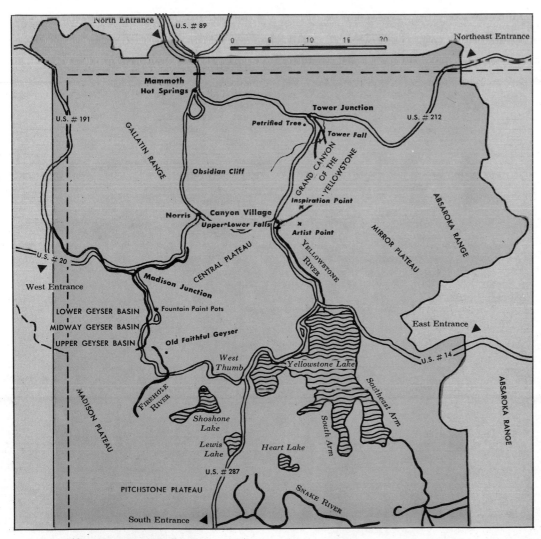

YELLOWSTONE NATIONAL PARK

The American elk (wapiti) is the largest deer in the United States. He makes a far-carrying bugle sound.

Trumpeter swan stay at Yellowstone all year because the water is heated from hot springs and geysers.

The thermal activity of the Norris Geyser Basin includes a variety of small geysers plus the violent and unpredictable Steamboat Geyser which has hurled steam and water as high as 300 feet into the air.

YOSEMITE

LOCATION: East-Central California
SIZE: 758,659 acres
ESTABLISHED: 1890

Long recognized for beauty and scenic resources, Yosemite has been protected for over 100 years. Known for variety — glaciated peaks and domes, high mountain falls, giant sequoias and subalpine meadows—Yosemite is the epitome of a national park. Rising 3,600 feet above Merced River in the Yosemite Valley is El Capitan, a granite monolith.

The dawn sun lies poised over Yosemite National Park, then the murmuring thunder of Bridalveil Creek seems to bring forth the hushed melody of the early morning wind blowing through spires of the groves of sequoias and evergreens as life stirs in this idyllic retreat in the High Sierra of California.

Whatever the season, winter of great snow or the pinnacle of summer, Yosemite lives on, its shape infinitely changing under the slow but persistent hand of nature.

Yosemite was born a hundred million years ago, but she carries her age with grace, growing more desirable with the millenniums. The Sierra Nevada gave birth to her, quaking with the pains of labor as the granite mass rose higher to the east, creating streams which drained into the Merced River.

The Merced grew in strength, not unlike a giant artery, flowing toward the San Joaquin Valley to cut a canyon 2,000 feet deep in the rolling upland surface. In Yosemite's puberty, the glaciers came, gouging the V-shaped canyon into a wider and deeper U-shaped trough.

Bridalveil was one of the creeks — Yosemite and Ribbon were others — which lost their lower extremities to the mighty glaciers, leaving the valleys hanging. These streams then plummeted into the valley. Then the glaciers melted, leaving hundreds of tons of water behind a moraine, or a natural dam of rock debris, forming a lake which in time became filled with silt, sand and rock to form the level valley floor we see today.

The wonders of Yosemite range from the awesome crash of water to canyons far below to the pastoral silence of flower-flocked meadowlands.

Congress saw its great beauty in 1864, and granted it to the State of California. In 1890 the national park was created around this Yosemite Grant. California ended its control of the grant in 1905, turning it back over to the Federal Government to form an enlarged national park. There are now nearly 1,200 square miles for all to enjoy, protected forever against the encroachment of man and his penchant for reshaping the face of nature.

But man has not just recently discovered Yosemite. The Ahwahneechee Indians lived here long before it was discovered by the white man. Their name for it, taken from the tribal description, was Ahwahnee, or "deep, grassy valley in the heart of the sky mountains."

A doe and her fawn nibble the grass in one of the four distinct life zones at Yosemite National Park.

Then, a little over a hundred years ago, the Mariposa Battalion, a band of miners, entered the valley, seeking retribution for Indian raids. Some of the miners, awed by the expansive beauty of the region, argued around a campfire, trying to name their surroundings. They finally agreed on "Yosemite," perhaps meaning "grizzly bear." It was a derivation of U-zu-ma-ti, the name of a sub-group of Chief Tenaya's tribe, who then inhabited the valley.

While the Mariposa Battalion's visit was the first recorded trip by white men, it is believed the Joseph Walker party touched on part of the park in their journey of 1833. Nonetheless, to the growing nation just beginning to discover itself in those few short years before the Civil War, Yosemite enthralled the young country.

Members of the battalion wrote enthusiastically of Yosemite, and four years later, in 1855, James M. Hutchings brought the first tourist party. This group would, a shade over a hundred years later, be only a millionth of Yosemite's annual visitors.

Hutchings, the publisher of *California Magazine*, wrote glowing articles extolling the natural virtues of

Yosemite, then where words failed, illustrated his pieces with sketches by Thomas Ayres. Hutchings' eloquent prose was reprinted by other publications, and soon Americans came to see for themselves. Californians, spirited by the great wonder which had been left in their midst, became concerned over Yosemite's future. In 1864, President Abraham Lincoln signed the Yosemite Grant, ceding it to California, to be held "inalienable for all time."

Thus, Yosemite became the first public park to be administered by a state government, and dictated the concept which has since served as the basis for the current National Park System.

It was fitting that this splendid region be such a first. There are hundreds of miles of trails leading from the valley through the coolness and fragrance of deep woods; across the sun-splashed meadows to high mountain lakes teeming with fish growing fat and ferocious in their chill depths.

But let us start at the valley, seven square miles of cragginess that becomes beautiful at once to the beholder. Mountainsides and cliffs overhang the canyon where the Merced River threads. A few miles

Upper and Lower Yosemite Falls (above) have a total drop of 2,425 feet. Tuolumne Meadows (below) is the largest subalpine meadow found in the High Sierra.

later, the roadway widens to a flower-flecked meadow, dominated by El Capitan, a flawless granite monolith rising more than 3,600 feet toward the sky. Nearly as imposing are the Cathedral Spires, Sentinel Rock and the Three Brothers named for the sons of Chief Tenaya whose domain this land once was.

Water shaped Yosemite, and still is slowly wearing away rock as it must, seeking the lower levels and carrying with it bits of stone and vegetable matter, endlessly creating. The Upper Yosemite Fall drops 1,430 feet, and the Lower a bit less than a fourth of that. Water cascades with a roar over the top of cliffs for a total drop of 2,425 feet from the crest of the Upper Fall to the base of the Lower.

Not all is the sound and fury of nature. There is solitude in Yosemite to be found in her stands of sequoias, one, the Grizzly Giant, believed to have been born from seed more than 3,000 years ago. This magnificent cousin of the redwood is 209 feet tall and is more than 34 feet in diameter across the base. Growing silently, contributing to its grandeur, are the park's incense-filled forests of pine and fir and cedar and oaks, providing habitat for band-tailed pigeons, pygmy owls, chipmunks and squirrels.

Deer and bear pause to feed here, then move on to the high country, a land of lakes and meadows, capped by high peaks casting great dark shadows on the rainbow of wildflowers below. Tuolumne Meadows at 8,600 feet is the largest subalpine meadow in the High Sierra. Though it can be best enjoyed on foot, there are auto roads leading to jewel-like Tenaya Lake and Tioga Pass, between granite bolders polished to a shine by the glaciers and past high domes of the same stone. Another road leads from the valley 30 miles to Glacier Point, giving a panoramic view of the High Sierra and the valley 3,300 feet below.

In spring, there is a flood of color—brilliant yellows and soft blues with the dark green of the conifers filling the eye with the splendor of an untouched land. In winter, the high country is forbidding when giant snows fill the land, only to melt into the trickle of mountain streams which become the raging torrent to start life anew in this land of 10,000 wonders.

John Muir, the great Scots-born naturalist, saw its contrasts: "the most songful streams in the world . . . the noblest forests . . . the loftiest granite domes . . . the deepest ice-sculptured canyons."

The Merced River drops over 900 feet when it reaches the 594-foot drop at Nevada Fall followed quickly by a 317-foot plunge at Vernal Fall. Seen from Glacier Point, Half Dome's bald face is to the left.

Bridalveil Fall drops between the Cathedral Rocks 620 feet, often swaying from frequent gusts of wind.

Two views of Half Dome: From Tenaya Creek the 8,852-foot-high dome (above) rises majestically. From Mirror Lake (below), a bald Mt. Watkins stands directly in front of Half Dome.

*L*embert Dome (left), in the Toulumne Meadows, unlike Half Dome, was polished by glacial action. Half Dome and others were formed by exfoliation, the cracking and expansion of rock layers which round off angular surfaces. The total immensity of Upper and Lower Yosemite Falls (right), seen in the background on page 203, is revealed by a close-up from a tree-lined road leading from Yosemite Village.

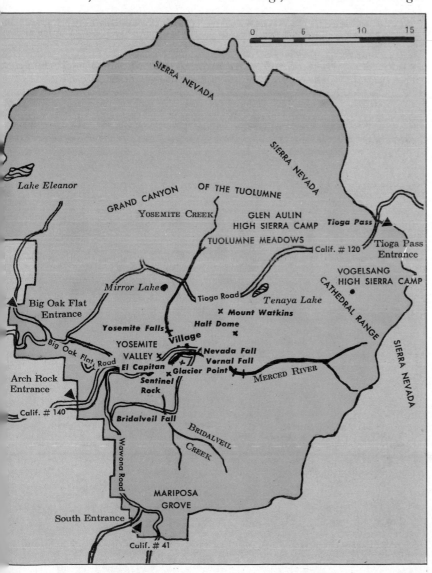

YOSEMITE NATIONAL PARK

Canyonland in color." That is Zion National Park in Utah which Mormon pioneers, in 1858, called a place of "peace and comfort," articulating the grandeur of infinite being which its 135,256 acres overwhelmingly suggests.

Ranging across the plateau and canyon region of southwestern Utah, the park's sheer-wall formations in color are unique among the world's geological phenomena. Over 150 million years of natural processes formed all this beauty. Here, visitors can actually follow the path of the large three-toed dinosaur and discern his huge footprints in hard sandstone rock layers. His distant cousins in the form of reptiles and amphibians still abound, yet the only deadly survivor of ages past, there in the park, is that dramatic insurgent of pioneer life, the rattlesnake.

Thirteen million years ago, the area, long a bottom for surging and subsiding seas, was lifted thousands of miles through phenomena such as mile-high deposits of sediment. The erosion of this uplifted plateau formed the domes, peaks and canyons that now have become familiar.

The native inhabitants of this region, the peaceful Paiute Indians, first looked upon the white man during the Escalante-Dominguez explorations in 1776. Fifty years later, Jedediah Smith led a party of trappers and fur traders into previously inaccessible reaches near this region, prowling and plodding in quest of pelts from Great Salt Lake south though the valleys probably to the Virgin River.

The gallant and intrepid Captain John C. Fremont, in his 1843-1844 explorations of the great Southwest, garnered the geographic certainties of primeval wonder which were to excite the imagination and determination of dedicated Mormon pioneers in 1847. Within a decade the Mormons had settled around the Virgin River and named the region, appropriately, Zion, "the heavenly city of God."

Major John Wesley Powell explored the region in 1872 and named the canyon of the north fork of the Virgin River "Munkuntuweap" and the canyon of the east fork "Parunuweap," Indian designations influencing the earliest identity of the park as a national monument in 1909. But the prevailing Mormon

ZION

LOCATION: Southwestern Utah
SIZE: 135,256 acres
ESTABLISHED: 1919

Rising above the Virgin River is Angels Landing, a sandstone monolith which is representative of the name Zion, the heavenly city of God. A stiff climb on foot and horse trails provides an excellent view of Zion Canyon from this 1,500-foot perch.

influence and flavor wrought the change to Zion National Park, and also its expansions in 1937 and 1956.

Greenery tumbles richly about the banks of the Virgin, contrasting breathtakingly with the majestic red of Navajo sandstone precipices and the intense blue of the skies overhead. To the northwest can be seen Horse Ranch Mountain, 8,740 feet high, towering above all the great cliffs of the park.

East of the highway, driving north along the effervescent north fork of the Virgin River, the Watchman, 6,555 feet, glows like a vast reddish-brown jewel in the glints and starts of a remorseless sun. The driver-distracting panorama continues up Zion Canyon, a distance of eight miles, to the Temple of Sinawava. To the left, in succession, are the reverently named heights: the Towers of The Virgin, the Altar of Sacrifice, the Beehives, Sentinel Peak, the Three Patriarchs, Majestic Mountain and Angels Landing; to the right, East Temple, Mount Spry, the Twin Brothers, Mountain of the Sun, Red Arch Mountain and the Great White Throne.

Beyond the Great White Throne, river and road twist to the west at The Organ, behind which Angels Landing rises 1,500 feet above canyon bed. Cable Mountain is on the right, now. A 6,496 foot peak, it takes its name from a 2,136-foot cable, used by lumbermen in 1900 to transport lumber from the east rim into the canyon. To the west is Cathedral Mountain with Observation Point and The Pulpit, soaring to the right and left. At the Temple of Sinawava the road ends, yielding to a trail toward The Narrows. Here the canyon narrows to a 1,500 foot chasm only a few feet wide and with sheerness of cliff pressing the hiker closely on both sides.

Zion Canyon has well been called a threshold or point of departure. It is only a beginning, for trails lead out of the canyon onto the highland plateau and far into the back country where unviolated wilderness is supreme. Paramount, and especially unique to Zion and its far reaches, is the instant understanding of Henry Van Dyke's phrase: "A national park should be as sacred as a temple."

Trails lead to overlooks, too, such as the one atop Angels Landing or to Observation Point at the end of the East Rim Trail. Here, as almost everywhere in Zion is what Enos Mills called "glorious room—room in which to find ourselves, in which to think and hope, to dream and plan, to rest and resolve."

From here the view of Zion Canyon offers a

unique geologic insight into the whole Zion region. Far below lies the meandering Virgin River, tortuous in its windings around each bend of rock on its way to Lake Mead of the Colorado.

The Virgin River is responsible for the inch by inch, eternal and incessant carving of Zion Canyon. The river has never been much larger than it is today and this is a clue to the fact that the river and its tributaries are not a fisherman's paradise — although fishing is permitted in the park. Frequent flooding and shiftings of silt and sand are not kind to the survival of trout in the stream and its offshoots.

Animals indigenous to the mountains and arid areas survive in this region, and the cough of the cougar, the chilly plaint of the coyote can be heard on the land. Bobcats, foxes, weasels, squirrels and chipmunks are numerous. Here the golden eagle and hawk are king and princeling among the feather-bearers. The wiry species of road-runner, spurred towhee, Rocky Mountain nuthatch, are extremely deft in avoiding the two aforementioned "dive-bombers" of the peaks.

The piñon pine, gnarled juniper, deep-green forests of Douglas and white fir flourish. And the golden aspen of autumn flourishes when moisture and soil are plentiful. Here are found the magical night-flowers, the jimson weed (or thornapple), the white-evening primrose and the ferns and grasses rich along the river and trickling streams.

In winter only the higher trails are unnegotiable because of snow. The contrasts of red sandstone amid blinding sun glancing off snow drifts can be productive of bizarre loveliness to behold. And in spring the cascades plummet in foaming furies over the sheer faces of the cliffs.

Such is Zion, the bequest of forgotten, prehistoric seas. "A great reservoir," as Donald Culross Peattie once wrote, "of the serene order of nature."

Cycles of geology for 150 million years — slow uplifting, vast seas, violent earth upheavals, weather and erosion — are responsible for such fascinating formations at Zion as the Great White Throne (opposite) and the Three Patriarchs (below). Both rise as part of the walls of Zion Canyon and can be seen on trips of varying lengths on foot or horse trails.

*B*obcats *(left), although they can climb very well, generally do so only for food or out of fear. Checkerboard Mesa (opposite, below) was formed when wind-blown sands laid cross-bedded deposits which were later cemented by a great sea. A changing panorama of multicolored cliffs rise from the floor of Zion Canyon (opposite, above). The Towers of the Virgin (above) is one of many sights with a reverent name. From Angels Landing (overleaf) one looks 1,500 feet straight down to the Virgin River and parallel road.*

215

EPILOGUE

Many of today's problems revolve around the challenge of re-establishing significant ties between today's urban man and his largely forgotten natural heritage.

It is obvious that land acquisition for parks and wilderness cannot keep up with an indefinitely expanding population. Open spaces, by the ineluctable force of economics, will be filled one day with subdivisions, office buildings, factories, freeways and parking lots. The American public cannot compete everywhere with overweening private demands.

Even assuming that some parks and parcels of wilderness can be held against the pressures of increasing numbers of people, the only way of preserving them would be to do what we do with any commodity in short supply — ration it. A wilderness trampled by thousands of refugees from the city is no longer a wilderness, and the only way it can be maintained in its natural state as the population increases is to keep people out — to limit access. You would make reservations and wait your turn — it would be as simple as that. That is what happens already in some crowded smaller countries.

Park and wilderness rationing in this country is not merely a prospect for the remote future, but could conceivably become necessary in the years or decades immediately ahead. To get in the car when the mood strikes you and find natural sanctuary from the pressures of modern life, as we do at present, may become a privilege to look back on, in the years to come, as we customarily look back on "Golden Ages" of the past.

We must be continually alert not only to ways of assuring ourselves and our children some daily and continuing contact with the land, but also to bring more beauty into our cities and to achieve a better kind of city and a better way of life. In his message to the Conference on Natural Beauty, President Johnson called for a "new conservation" not only to protect the countryside and save it from destruction but to restore what has been destroyed and salvage the beauty and charm of our growing cities.

The park service is not only responsible for protecting national parks and national seashores. Because of its important involvement in historic preservation, the National Park Service has recently returned to the forefront of city planning and is pioneering in many conservation projects in close cooperation with city planners. One of these continuing projects has been the National Historic Landmarks Program to identify and encourage protection of many of the nation's finest remaining examples of our historic heritage in towns and cities all over the nation. In at least five major cities, the National Park Service administers historical areas of great national significance which also serve as important cases of open space in crowded metropolitan centers.

Perhaps our closest identification with city planning has been in the nation's capital itself. The Washington showcase demonstrates perhaps better than any other American city, just what can be done when parks and open green spaces are woven into the very fabric of metropolitan life.

We must think of our total environment — not simply in the context of the house we own or the block we live in or the office where we work — but in the web of relationships that links all flowerboxes, all gardens, all parks, all towns — and the spaces in between. My own view of the new conservation is that from this point on, *there is only one environment*. Resources are all interrelated and the old fashioned idea of conservation of saving bits and pieces here and there is outdated.

Since 75 per cent of our people live in urban areas and they must have water and air in order to exist, we had better address ourselves to the total problem — which is the problem of the overall environment. Otherwise, much of our effort in natural resource management will be misdirected and some of our decisions will be unwise. For this reason, I am pleased that the people in the Department of Housing and Urban Development are beginning to regard themselves as conservationists and take just as much interest in our problems as we take in theirs.

The atmosphere moves and water moves and pollution is everywhere, and we either face up to the big problem and work at it together or we don't really achieve the conservation objectives that we have in mind.

Modern science is a coin that has both a bright side and a dark side. The very science that can teach us to renew can, if misdirected, cause us to waste, plunder and poison the world of nature that is our home.

The pollution of water and air is the conservation scandal of the 1960's in the United States. Today, some large American rivers are little more than running sewers; and the air over some cities is so dangerously contaminated as to threaten human health. In recent years we have gained new momentum and a new sense of direction in our fight against waste and pollution and blight. But much work remains to be done.

What will happen to the quality of life as we approach the point where the available natural areas of the continent offer standing room only? As population crowds in on us, it will surely be the kind of unique experience offered by wilderness that is sacrificed first. There will still be available the kind of outdoor experience that can be enjoyed today at amusement parks on the Fourth of July. And this may, indeed, be the only kind of outdoor experience available if we race blindly ahead down the road of "growth and progress."

We can only guess what will happen to the individual

as the pressures of overcrowding increasingly bear down on him, as the subtle diseases of overcivilization take their toll on his mind and body. It may be that in the long run, overpopulation of our own country will be a grave threat to the most important freedom of all — the freedom each person must have to maintain his own integrity, to be true to his natural self.

City-bound youngsters in particular need the blessing of an available out-of-doors, a daily contact with nature in playgrounds and little parks within skipping distance of their homes. They need access to beaches. They need places close, yet removed, where they can walk. They need a place to hunt lizards or to discover an aspen leaf quivering in a faint breeze.

When the last census showed that the State of Vermont had not gained in population, Senator George Aiken was heard to remark "When we look at what's happening in other parts of the country we're not disturbed — we'll wait and grow right."

What does it mean to "grow right?" I would say it means, among other things, to grow in such a way as to leave room for the quality experience, particularly in nature. It is to grow in such a way that our grandchildren will still be able to see in some places the natural shapes of the land, will be able to find surcease from the tensions of modern life among the God-given forms of mountains and trees and streams and unspoiled beaches.

Unlike many countries of Europe and Asia that have used up all their vacant lands, we still have an option in America. We still have open space and wild lands to preserve — lands that still exist in their pristine splendor or something close to it. Let us then make the choice intelligently as free men considering the welfare of future generations.

One of America's great contributions to the world has been the national park idea, the principle of preserving for all time, future generations willing, the finest of our scenic forests and deserts and mountains and shorelines.

I am suggesting that if this magnificent principle is not to be lost in the chaos of unplanned growth, it is time for us to take a further step. I am suggesting that the United States set an example of how to plan the best relationship of human beings to their environment, that we give solemn attention to the matter of developing the optimum man-land ratio — the ratio which would result not only in the "highest and best use" of the land, but the highest and best development of free men.

We can begin by asking the right questions: What is the ideal relationship of men to nature? What is the optimum population for a given environment? How can we maintain the quality of life and not be submerged by quantity?

The need today is to establish enough of each kind of outdoor recreation opportunity to satisfy public pressures without destroying the resources. But setting aside these areas is not enough. Another generation, if untutored and unappreciative of the deeper meaning of this green legacy, might well stand idly by, allowing destruction of the basic natural values of these hard-won parks. The great conservationist Aldo Leopold once said: " . . . Recreational development is a job not of building roads into lovely country, but of building receptivity into the still unlovely human mind."

Each generation is tempted to promote its own prosperity by drawing on the resource bank of future generations. Should we not resolve here to use our full influence to see that this nation makes decisions that ensure a handsome deposit in the resource bank of our children?

APPENDIX

I Basic Information on National Parks

ACADIA
(Maine)

Park Season
Park campgrounds, picnic areas and other facilities are open from about May 10 to October 15.

Getting to Acadia
By automobile: Turn off U.S. 1 at Ellsworth onto Maine Route 3 to Bar Harbor, and other Mount Desert Island towns. Greyhound buses serve Bar Harbor daily all year.

Accommodations
The park has two campgrounds, at Black Woods and Seawall. Trailers are welcome but there are no utility connections for them. Summer hotels and roominghouses are located in villages on Mount Desert Island and in towns near Schoodic Peninsula.

BIG BEND
(Texas)

Park Season
The park is open all year.

Getting to Big Bend
By automobile: From San Antonio and points east, take U.S. 90 to Marathon (39 miles away from the park), then turn south onto U.S. 385. From Alpine (80 miles away) and points west and north, take Texas Route 118. Alpine and Marathon are served by buses, from the east and west by Continental Trailways, and from the north by Trans-Pecos. There is no regular public transportation to the park.

Accommodations
The Basin, where lodge, motel and cottages are available, is the only place inside the park that has overnight accommodations. Campgrounds are located at the Basin and Rio Grande Village. There are trailer sites with utility connections at Panther Junction and Rio Grande Village. Hotels and motels are located at Alpine and Marathon.

BRYCE CANYON
(Utah)

Park Season
The park is open to visitors all year, but facilities for tourists, such as cabins, stores and cafeterias are closed from October to May. The park road is open in winter to Sunset Point, Inspiration Point, Bryce Point and Paria View.

Getting to Bryce Canyon
By automobile: From the North Rim of Grand Canyon National Park (140 miles away) and points south, take

(Continued on page 220)

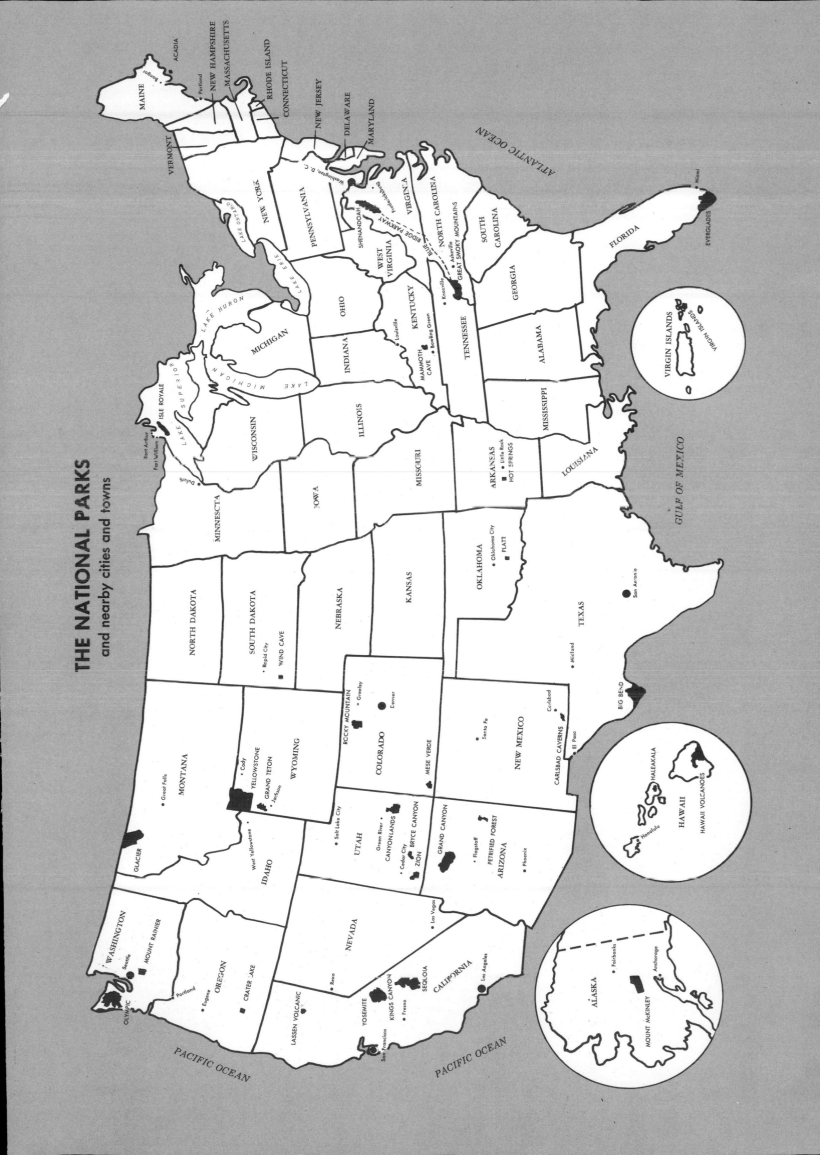

THE NATIONAL PARKS
and nearby cities and towns

Arizona Route 67 to Jacob Lake, Arizona, turn north onto U.S. Alternate 89-U.S. 89, take to Bryce Junction in Utah, then turn east onto Utah Route 12. From Salt Lake City (267 miles away) and points north, take U.S. 89 to Utah Route 12. Buses operate from Salt Lake City and Los Angeles to Cedar City, where Utah Parks Co. buses connect with the park.

Accommodations

There are two types of cabins available at the Lodge, near the rim of Bryce Amphitheater, which is open from about June 10 to Labor Day. Deluxe cabins are built of logs or stone and have a fireplace; standard cabins can accommodate two families in one two-unit structure. Cabins are also available through the Inn and the Store, which are near the North Campground. There are two campgrounds, North Campground and Sunset Campground. Camping facilities for tents and trailers are available from May 15 to October 15.

CANYONLANDS
(Utah)

Park Season

The park is open all year.

Getting to Canyonlands

By automobile: There are two entrances from U.S. 160: *Island in the Sky District:* Turn from U.S. 160, 17 miles north of Moab; take road 22 miles to the park. *Needles District:* Turn from U.S. 160, 41 miles south of Moab; take road 34 miles to park.

Accommodations

There are no overnight accommodations within the park, the nearest being in Monticello (southeast of the park) and Moab (northeast of the park), both on U.S. 160. There are campgrounds at Squaw Flat and other primitive campsites are available.

CARLSBAD CAVERNS
(New Mexico)

Park Season

The park is open all year. The evening bat flights occur from May to October.

Getting to Carlsbad Caverns

By automobile: From Carlsbad (about 27 miles away) and points east, take U.S. 62-U.S. 180. From points north, take U.S. 285 to Carlsbad. From El Paso (about 150 miles away) and points west, take U.S. 62-U.S. 180. Carlsbad Caverns Coaches serve the park from both cities.

Accommodations

There are no overnight accommodations within the park but hotels, motels, trailer courts and campgrounds are in Carlsbad and White's City, as well as along the approach highways.

CRATER LAKE
(Oregon)

Park Season

The park is open all year although the campgrounds are closed from September 30 to about July 1, depending on snow conditions. Cabins are closed from September 10 to about June 15. North Entrance Road is open by about mid-June, the Rim Drive by early July.

Getting to Crater Lake

By automobile: The following highways connect with entrances: *West Entrance:* From Medford (69 miles away), take Oregon Route 62. *South Entrance:* From U.S. 97, take Oregon Route 62. *North Entrance:* From U.S. 97, take Oregon Route 138. During the summer buses operate from Medford and Klamath Falls to Crater Lake.

Accommodations

Lodge and cabins are located at Rim Village. Among the campgrounds are: Mazama and Annie Spring, near the junction of South and West Entrance Roads, Lost Creek, on the road to the Pinnacles and Rim Village. Trailers are welcome but there are no utility connections.

EVERGLADES
(Florida)

Park Season

The park is open all year.

Getting to Everglades

By automobile: From Miami (about 30 miles away) and points north, take U.S. 1 to Florida City, then take Florida Route 27.

Accommodations

Overnight accommodations, campsites for 344, marina supplies and services are available. Boats up to 100 feet long can be accommodated. Camping space is available at Long Pine Key (6 miles from park entrance) or Flamingo Campground and in the back country at designated locations.

GLACIER
(Montana)

Park Season

The main travel season is from June 15 to September 10, when the major hotels and cabin-camps are open. The Going-to-the-Sun Road is usually open from June 1 to October 15 if weather permits.

Getting to Glacier

By automobile: From Great Falls (140 miles away) and points southeast, take U.S. 89 to Browning, then turn west onto U.S. 2 to East Glacier Park, then turn north onto Montana Route 49, take for 4 miles to junction with entrance road. From points west, take U.S. 2. From Missoula (154 miles away) and points south, take U.S. 93 to Kalispell, then turn east onto U.S. 2. The Intermountain Transportation Co. operates buses to West Glacier from Missoula on the south and to East Glacier Park from Shelby and Great Falls to the east.

Accommodations

Many Glacier Hotel and Lake McDonald and Glacier Park Lodges are in or near the park (open from about June 15 to September 10). Motels and cabins are available at Swiftcurrent, Rising Sun and Apgar Village. Major campgrounds are located at Apgar, Sprague Creek, Avalanche Creek, St. Mary, Rising Sun, Swiftcurrent and Two Medicine. Trailer space is available at all campgrounds except Sprague Creek but without utility connections.

GRAND CANYON
(Arizona)

Park Season

The road into the park at the *North Rim* is usually blocked with snow by November 1 and remains closed until early May. The *South Rim* of the park is open all year.

Getting to Grand Canyon

By automobile: *North Rim:* From points north, take U.S. 89 and/or U.S. Alternate 89 to Jacob Lake, then turn south onto Arizona Route 67. There is bus service from Cedar City, Utah, only from mid-June through August. *South Rim:* From Flagstaff (73 miles away) and U.S. 66, take U.S. 180 north to Arizona Route 64, then turn north. Buslines serve Grand Canyon Village from Williams and Flagstaff.

Accommodations

North Rim: Accommodations at the campground, Grand Canyon Lodge and North Rim Inn are available only in summer. *South Rim:* El Tovar Hotel, Yavapai Lodge, Bright Angel Lodge and cabins are among the accommodations. Campgrounds are maintained at Grand Canyon Village and at Desert View. The Trailer Village has utility hookups.

Grand Canyon National Monument

Adjoining the park on the west is Grand Canyon National Monument, a primitive area of about 310 square miles established in 1932. At Toroweap Point is one of the most impressive views in the canyon. Looking straight down the sheer rock walls, one can see the snake-like Colorado River, 3,000 feet below, a view not possible in Grand Canyon National Park. To the west is Mount Trumbull, the last landmark of the Grand Canyon country on the western horizon.

GRAND TETON
(Wyoming)

Park Season

The fullest operation of the park facilities is from early June through Labor Day. Roads are open from the town of Jackson through the park and over Togwotee Pass throughout the winter.

Getting to Grand Teton

By automobile: From points east, take U.S. 287-U.S. 26. From points south (Jackson), take U.S. 89-U.S. 187-U.S. 26. From Victor, Idaho, and points west, take Wyoming Route 22 (Idaho Route 33). From South Entrance of Yellowstone National Park (6 miles away) and points north, take U.S. 89-U.S. 287. By bus, from Victor, Idaho, take Grand Teton Lodge Company buses. From Yellowstone National Park, there is daily bus service to Jackson Lake Lodge. From Rock Springs, Wyoming, take Jackson-Rock Springs Stages to Jackson.

Accommodations

Main campgrounds are at Colter Bay, Lizard Point, Signal Mountain, Jenny

Lake and Gros Ventre River. An overflow campground is located at Pilgrim Creek. Trailers are permitted in all campgrounds except Jenny Lake, but no utilities are available. There is a daily utility fee at the concession operated Colter Bay Trailer Village. The organized group campground is at Colter Bay. Jackson Lake Lodge has rooms and a large cottage colony. There are cabins at Colter Bay and Jenny Lake Lodge. Lodges and guest ranches are scattered throughout the park.

GREAT SMOKY
(North Carolina and Tennessee)

Park Season
The park is open all year.

Getting to Great Smoky Mountains
By automobile: From Knoxville, Tennessee (39 miles away) and points west and north, take U.S. 441. From Asheville, North Carolina (49 miles away) and points south and east, take U.S. 19 to Blue Ridge Parkway. Buses cross the park seven times daily between Knoxville and Asheville via Cherokee, North Carolina, and Gatlinburg, Tennessee.

Accommodations
Le Conte Lodge, accessible only by foot or horse trail, offers (during summer months only) the only concessioner-operated accommodations within the park. The park contains 15 summer campgrounds, but campground facilities are limited during other months. Trailers are permitted, but no electric or sewer connections are available. Hotels and motels are in nearby towns and cities.

HALEAKALA
(Hawaii)

Park Season
The park is open all year.

Getting to Haleakala
Passenger planes from Honolulu to Island of Maui (where park is located) make scheduled flights several times daily. From Kahului Airport on Maui, the distance to the park is 26 miles by Hawaii Routes 37, 377 and 378. Tour cars for rent are available from airport.

Accommodations
Other than one campground along the park road and three cabins within the crater (at Kapalaoa, Paliku and Holua), no overnight accommodations are available. Camping and picnicking facilities are maintained at Hosmer Grove at the edge of park.

HAWAII VOLCANOES
(Hawaii)
Park Season
The park is open all year.
Getting to Hawaii Volcanoes
Airlines make scheduled flights from Honolulu several times daily to Hilo (on east side of Hawaii Island) and to Kailua-Kona (on west side). Car rentals, taxis and tour buses are available at these two points.

Accommodations
There are three overnight campgrounds

and two equipped overnight resthouses for hikers. The latter are on Mauna Loa, one at 10,000 feet and one at the summit, which is 13,680 feet, where Mokuaweoweo Caldera is located.

HOT SPRINGS
(Arkansas)

Park Season
The park is open all year.

Getting to Hot Springs
By automobile: From Little Rock (56 miles away) and points northeast, take U.S. 30 to U.S. 70. From points southeast (Pine Bluff, 71 miles away) or from points northwest, take U.S. 270. From points southwest, take U.S. 70. From points south or north, take Arkansas Route 7. Arkansas Motor Coaches, Continental Trailways, Wolf and Midwest Buslines operate to Hot Springs.

Accommodations
The City of Hot Springs has many hotels (the largest accommodating more than 1,000 guests), motels, kitchenette and standard apartments, and cottages. Within the park there is a campground in Gulpha Gorge at the foot of the eastern slope of Hot Springs Mountain. Trailer sites do not have utility hookups.

ISLE ROYALE
(Michigan)

Park Season
The park is officially open from May 1 through November 1.

Getting to Isle Royale
From late June through Labor Day, daily boat service is available from Grand Portage, Minnesota (22 miles away) to Windigo Inn on southwest end of the island; and from Copper Harbor, Michigan (56 miles away), to Rock Harbor Lodge on northeast end of the island. During the same period, the National Park Service boat leaves Houghton, Michigan (73 miles away), Tuesday, Thursday and Saturday for Rock Harbor Lodge. From May through October, the Voyageur (operated by the Siverston Bros. Fisheries, Duluth) makes two or three trips weekly to and from Grand Portage, circumnavigating the island. Arrangements can be made to have it pick up visitors at any lakeside campground.

Accommodations
Rock Harbor Lodge and Windigo Inn operate from June 20 to Labor Day. There are 22 lakeside campgrounds.

LASSEN VOLCANIC
(California)

Park Season
Although roads are closed by snow from about the end of October to June 1, the park is officially open all year. However, the road to the ski area near the Southwest Entrance Station is open all year.

Getting to Lassen Volcanic
By automobile: From Redding (52 miles away) to Manzanita Lake (Northwest Entrance), take California Route 44. From Mount Shasta City (100 miles

away) to Manzanita Lake, take California Route 89. From Red Bluff (52 miles away) to Southwest Entrance, take California Route 36. From Susanville (69 miles away) to Southwest Entrance, take California Route 36. Buses operate from Red Bluff and Susanville to Mineral (12 miles away) all year, from Redding to Manzanita Lake from June 15 to September 15.

Accommodations
Overnight accommodations within the park are available from June 10 to the end of October. These include Manzanita Lake Lodge located one-half mile from the Manzanita Lake (Northwest) Entrance, nearby houskeeping and deluxe cabins and hotel bungalows. Depending on snow conditions, most of the park's eight campgrounds are open from the end of June to the end of September. Some of the campsites (out of a total of 600) are open at Manzanita Lake from May 1 to October 15. Skiing facilities are in operation near the Southwest Entrance from about Thanksgiving Day to the middle of April.

MAMMOTH CAVE
(Kentucky)

Park Season
The park is open all year.

Getting to Mammoth Cave
By automobile: From Louisville (100 miles away) and points north and east take U.S. 31W to Cave City, then take Kentucky Route 70 ten miles to park headquarters. From Nashville, Tennessee (100 miles away) and points south and west, take 31W through Bowling Green (32 miles away) to Park City, then take Kentucky Route 255 to park headquarters.

Accommodations
Mammoth Cave Hotel, which is within the park, has rooms with and without bath and is open all year. The motel-type lodge and electrically heated cottages are also open all year. Unheated cabins are available from May to September. The campground, with 143 sites, is open all year.

MESA VERDE
(Colorado)

Park Season
May 15 to October 15. From October 15 to May 15, however, the museum and one loop of the ruins road is open, and guided trips are conducted into one cliff dwelling, weather permitting.

Getting to Mesa Verde
The park entrance is located between Cortez (9 miles east) and Durango, Colorado (38 miles west), on U.S. 160. It is 21 miles from the park entrance to park headquarters. Continental Trailways operates buses to the park from Durango from May 15 to October 15.

Accommodations
The Mesa Verde Company provides overnight accommodations at Spruce Tree Lodge and at Far View Annex between early May and October 15. The campground is open during non-freezing weather, approximately from May 1

to November 1 and limited camping facilities are maintained during the winter. Trailer sites do not include utility hook-ups.

MOUNT McKINLEY
(Alaska)

Park Season
The single terminal road is open normally from about June 1 to September 10.

Getting to Mount McKinley
Denali Highway, the only road to the park, connects with the Richardson Highway at Paxson, 160 miles away. There is a 3,000-foot landing strip for private aircraft, and daily train service to the park from Anchorage and Fairbanks.

Accommodations
McKinley Park Hotel offers lodging. The park contains six campgrounds, but there are no housetrailer utilities. A small resort, Camp Denali, is just north of Wonder Lake, outside the park.

MOUNT RAINIER
(Washington)

Park Season
The roads from *Nisqually Entrance* to Paradise (where skiing activities are centered) and from the northeast boundary to Ohanapecosh are open all year, although snow conditions may cause them to be closed for short periods. Other roads are closed for the winter after the first heavy snowfall, usually about November 1. They are usually opened between June 15 and July 1.

Getting to Mount Rainier
By automobile: The following highways connect with the entrances: *White River Entrance* (northeast corner of park): From Tacoma (58 miles away) and points north, take U.S. 410. *Nisqually River Entrance* (southwest corner): From Tacoma (55 miles away), take Washington Route 7 to Washington Route 706. *Stevens Canyon Entrance* (southwest corner): From points east, south and west, take Washington Route 14 to Washington Route 143. From late June to early September, daily bus service is available from Tacoma and Seattle to Longmire and Paradise.

Accommodations
National Park Inn, at Longmire, is open from early May until October. Paradise Inn is open from late June until Labor Day. The main campgrounds are at Cougar Rock, Paradise, Ohanapecosh, White River and Sunrise. There are no utility hook-ups for housetrailers. The only campground open in winter is Sunshine Point.

OLYMPIC
(Washington)

Park Season
The park is open all year, although snow closes higher elevations from late fall to early spring.

Getting to Olympic
The main approach road to the park is U.S. 101, which may be reached from Seattle by ferry and toll bridge or from Olympia (36 miles away from nearest point) to the southeast and Aberdeen and Hoquiam (52 miles away from nearest point) on the coast to the southwest. Year-around ferry service is available across Strait of Juan de Fuca between Victoria, British Columbia, and Port Angeles, Washington, where park headquarters is located. Buses serve Port Angeles, Forks and Neah Bay on the west side of Olympic Peninsula.

Accommodations
Lodges and cabins are available inside and outside the park. There are 15 developed campgrounds. No utility connections for trailers are available in the campgrounds, but various trailer parks and some lodges offer utility connections.

PETRIFIED FOREST
(Arizona)

Park Season
The park is open during daylight hours all year.

Getting to Petrified Forest
By automobile: From points east, take U.S. 66. From points southwest, south and west take U.S. 180.

Accommodations
There are no overnight accommodations within the park, and camping is not allowed. Motels are located along the highways leading to the park and in nearby communities.

PLATT
(Oklahoma)

Park Season
The park is open all year.

Getting to Platt
By automobile: From points north and south, take U.S. 77 to Davis (9 miles away), then turn east onto Oklahoma Route 7. From points east and west, take U.S. 70 to Ardmore (32 miles away), then turn north onto U.S. 177. U.S. 177 crosses the park from south to north, connecting with U.S. 70 at the south and U.S. 66 at the north.

Accommodations
There are no hotels or cabins in the park; however, they are available in the adjacent town of Sulphur. Three large campgrounds provide more than 200 campsites. The largest, Rock Creek Campground, is located at extreme western end of the park; Cold Springs Campground is in east-central section.

ROCKY MOUNTAIN
(Colorado)

Park Season
The park is open all year, although Trail Ridge Road is closed from about mid-October until late May.

Getting to Rocky Mountain
By automobile: From Loveland (29 miles away) and points east, take U.S. 34. From Longmont (30 miles away) and points east take Colorado Route 66. From points west and south, take U.S. 40 to Granby, then take U.S. 34.

Accommodations
There are no overnight accommodations within the park, except a few that are on private land. The major campgrounds are located at Moraine Park, Glacier Basin, Aspenglen, Endovalley, Longs Peak, Wild Basin and Timber Creek. Housetrailers are permitted but there are no utility connections.

SEQUOIA and KINGS CANYON
(California)

Parks Seasons
The parks are open all year, although Generals Highway is closed by snow at times in winter.

Getting to Sequoia and Kings Canyon
The two main entrances to the parks are on the west side. By automobile: To *Big Stump Entrance, Kings Canyon;* from Fresno (52 miles away), take California Route 180. From Visalia (47 miles away), take California Routes 198 and 69. To *Ash Mountain Entrance, Sequoia;* from Visalia (34 miles away), take California Route 198. Sightseeing buses operate from Tulare and Visalia to Giant Forest in summer.

Accommodations
Giant Forest Lodge is open from late May to Late October; Grant Grove Lodge from late May to mid-September. There are cabins at various locations; some are open all year, others only during late spring and summer. Most of the campgrounds are open from June 1 until closed by snow in October. There are no utility connections for trailers.

SHENANDOAH
(Virginia)

BLUE RIDGE PARKWAY
(North Carolina, Virginia)

SHENANDOAH

Park Season
The park is open all year.

Getting to Shenandoah
By automobile: the following highways connect with the entrances along Skyline Drive: *North Entrance* (Front Royal, Virginia): U.S. 340, Virginia Routes 55 and 522. *Thornton Gap* (31.6 miles from North Entrance): U.S. 211. *Swift Run Gap* (65.7 miles): U.S. 33. *South Entrance* (Rockfish Gap): U.S. 250 (Charlottesville, 25 miles away to the east) and the Blue Ridge Parkway.

Accommodations
Hotel-type accommodations and cabins within the park are closed from early November to mid-April. There are three modern campgrounds and another under construction.

BLUE RIDGE PARKWAY

Parkway Season
The parkway is open all year. Visitor facilities are open from May through October. Road is open except when hazardous driving conditions prevail; inquire locally.

Getting to Blue Ridge Parkway
The northern end of the parkway is reached from U.S. 250 or Skyline Drive,

with nearby connections from U.S. 340 and Virginia Routes 151, 6 and 664. The southern end of the parkway is reached from U.S. 441, with nearby connection from U.S. 19. The parkway is reached from major transmountain highways throughout its 469-mile length.

Accommodations

Hotel-type accommodations at three locations and nine parkway campgrounds are open from May through October. There are no utility connections for housetrailers.

VIRGIN ISLANDS
(St. John Island)

Park Season

The park is open all year.

Getting to Virgin Islands

Scheduled air and steamship lines give regular service to St. Thomas, by air about 4 hours from New York, 3 hours from Miami. Once on St. Thomas, taxis are available from the port city of Charlotte Amalie to Red Hook Landing, about 9 miles away, where scheduled commercial boats are available for the 30-minute passage to the park entrance at Cruz Bay on St. John.

Accommodations

The largest guest facility is Caneel Bay Plantation. A limited number of housekeeping cottages are also available on St. John. A campground is located at Cinnamon Bay.

WIND CAVE
(South Dakota)

Park Season

The cave is closed in winter, although one may drive through the park all year. Cave trips are conducted daily at scheduled intervals from April 1 through October 31.

Getting to Wind Cave

By automobile: From Hot Springs (10 miles away) and points south, take U.S. 385. From Custer (21 miles away) and points north, take U.S. 385. Also through Custer State Park, one of the largest state parks in the nation, take South Dakota Route 87. Transcontinental buses serve Hot Springs and Custer.

Accommodations

There are modern hotels, motels and trailer courts in Hot Springs and Custer and other nearby towns along approach highways to the park. Within the park, the campground, Elk Mountain, has trailer space, but no utility connections. It is open from mid-May until late September.

YELLOWSTONE
(Wyoming, Idaho and Montana)

Park Season

The park is open from May 1 to October 31.

Getting to Yellowstone

By automobile: The following highways connect with the entrances: West Entrance; U.S. 191 and 20. South Entrance; From Grand Teton National Park (6 miles away), U.S. 89 and 287. East Entrance; From Cody, Wyoming (53 miles away), U.S. 14 and 20. North Entrance; From Livingston, Montana (55 miles away), U.S. 89. Northeast Entrance; From Red Lodge, Montana, (64 miles away), U.S. 212.

Accommodations

Several hotels and lodges are available; also cabins and cottages. Main campgrounds are located at Mammoth Hot Springs, Madison Junction, Old Faithful, Grant Village, Bridge Bay, Fishing Bridge, Canyon Village, Norris, Lewis Lake, Indian Creek, Slough Creek, Tower Falls and Pebble Creek. There is a commercial trailer park at Fishing Bridge with water, electrical and sewage hookups.

YOSEMITE
(California)

Park Season

The park is open all year.

Getting to Yosemite

By automobile: The following highways connect with the entrances: Big Oak Flat Entrance (west side): From Stockton (130 miles away), take U.S. 99 to California Route 120. Arch Rock Entrance (southwest): From Merced (70 miles away), take California Route 140. South Entrance: From Fresno (90 miles away), take California Route 41. Tioga Pass Entrance (east side): From U.S. 395 (at Lee Vining), take California Route 120. The Yosemite Transportation System operates to Yosemite Valley from Fresno and Lake Tahoe in summer and from Merced all year.

Accommodations

There are several hotels and lodges available in the park, also cabins. Some 20 campgrounds have more than 3,800 sites. There are no utility connections for trailers except at one location on private property.

ZION
(Utah)

Park Season

The park is open all year, although higher trails become impassable in winter. Tours, guided walks and evening programs are in full operation only in summer.

Getting to Zion

Utah Route 15 enters the two main entrances, East Entrance and South Entrance. Route 15 connects with U.S. 89 on the east and U.S. 91 on the west.

Accommodations

Zion Lodge, located in the heart of Zion Canyon, is open from about June 15 through Labor Day. Zion Inn, which has cabins, is near the South Entrance; it is open from about May 15 to September 30. There are two campgrounds. South Campground with campsites and trailer sites is open all year. Watchman (new in 1967) and Grotto Campgrounds are open from May 30 to Labor Day.

GROSS ACREAGES OF THE NATIONAL PARKS

*(Figures below include non-Federally controlled land within park boundaries Acreages given in main text refer only to Federally controlled land. *Indicates all land within park is Federal land.)*

Acadia	41,634.01
Big Bend	708,221.20
Bryce Canyon*	36,010.38
Canyonlands*	257,640.00
Carlsbad Caverns	46,753.07
Crater Lake*	160,290.33
Everglades	1,400,533.00
Glacier	1,013,029.12
Grand Canyon	673,575.00
Grand Teton	310,350.18
Great Smoky Mountains	512,673.71
Haleakala	26,402.78
Hawaii Volcanoes	220,344.84
Hot Springs*	1,035.24
Isle Royale*	539,347.08
Kings Canyon	460,330.90
Lassen Volcanic	106,933.78
Mammoth Cave	51,354.40
Mesa Verde	52,073.62
Mount McKinley	1,939,493.00
Mount Rainier	241,983.00
Olympic	896,599.10
Petrified Forest*	94,289.33
Platt*	911.97
Rocky Mountain	262,324.22
Sequoia	386,862.97
Shenandoah	212,303.51
Virgin Islands	15,150.00
Wind Cave*	28,059.26
Yellowstone	2,221,772.61
Yosemite	760,951.10
Zion	147,034.97
TOTAL	13,826,167.68

II

Seven Proposed National Parks

The National Park System continues to grow. The most recent park to be established was Canyonlands National Park, Utah, founded in 1964. The next parks to be established will come from the following list of seven areas in six states, which have been proposed for national parks:

Proposed Channel Islands National Park — California

The northern group of the Channel Islands of California presents one of the finest opportunities in America to preserve a combination of island seashore and related marine values within a national park.

The islands' rugged yet inviting terrain and observation of a wide range of marinelife and mammals are some of the outdoor activities the islands offer. They also have a rich history. Juan Rodriguez Cabrillo, the first European to sight the California coast, 36 years after Columbus landed in the Caribbean Islands, spent the winter of 1542-1543 on San Miguel Island and is reportedly buried there.

The islands contain archeological and possibly paleontological values not elsewhere represented in the National Park System.

Isolated in some cases from the mainland for upwards of a half-million years, the plants and animals have evolved distinctive characteristics unknown elsewhere. Important colonies of sea elephants, sea lions and seals inhabit the islands. The undersea environment undisturbed by man needs protection for further marine biological research.

Not only do the islands form a great natural biological laboratory, they constitute a museum of geological structures and processes. In these now partly submerged mountains, are examples of faulting, volcanism, fossils, canyon development, stream piracy and erosion.

The park proposal of 132,000 acres of land would consist of a closely related group of five of the eight Channel Islands, and their surrounding waters situated from 10 to 50 miles off the coast of southern California. Included within the park would be Santa Barbara and Anacapa Island, now within the Channel Islands National Monument, and San Miguel, Santa Cruz and Santa Rosa Islands — the latter two being in private ownership and comprising approximately 117,000 acres.

Recent action by the Santa Barbara County Board of Supervisors will provide the opportunity for private developers to utilize portions of the area proposed for inclusion in the national park for their own commercial interests. Also, the State of California is considering the leasing of oil rights surrounding the Channel Islands. There is some concern that this activity may damage the on-shore and marine values associated with the island group.

Proposed Great Basin National Park — Nevada

The term "Great Basin" refers generally to an aggregation of about 100 separate basins and their associated mountains in which drainage generally never reaches the sea. It covers most of Nevada, the western half of Utah and sections of Oregon and California.

It is a land characterized by isolated mountain ranges separated by desert plains and valleys in which are found many unusual geologic forms and structures and varied plant and animal species. It is a land of contrasts. Within the proposed boundaries are found plant and animal life characteristic of five of the Seven Life Zones of the world. From the desert valleys, at approximately 7,000 feet in elevation, it ranges to the dominant feature of Wheeler Park, rising over a mile above the desert floor.

Geologic processes of mountain uplift, faulting, folding and overthrust rock metamorphosis and the work of glaciers are evident. A rock arch over 60 feet high rises in the Arch Canyon. Alpine lakes, as well as smaller lakes and streams at the lower elevations, lie within the area. Lehman Caves National Monument, with exceptionally fine cave formation, would be included within the park boundary. Mount Washington and the adjacent highlands contain the most extensive forest of bristlecone pine — among the oldest living plants on earth.

The park proposal would establish an area of approximately 123,360 acres in the southern half of the Snake Mountain Range, southeast of Ely, Nevada. Of the acreage recommended for inclusion within the boundary, 100 acres are owned by the state, about 2,100 acres are in private ownership and the remainder under Federal administration. The opposition to the park centers around the exclusion of mining, grazing and hunting interests.

There were two bills in the 89th Congress proposing the establishment of a Great Basin National Park. One for an area of 123,360 acres, the other for an area of 53,120 acres. The Department of Interior has recommended the adoption of the larger area to allow for protection of the scene, to maintain a reasonable balance of plants to animals which are a natural part of the scene, and, at the same time, provide for the development and public use of the area without endangering the basic value for which the area would be established.

Proposed Guadalupe Mountains National Park — Texas

The proposed Guadalupe Mountains National Park is located in west Texas adjacent to the Texas-New Mexico state line, about 110 miles east of El Paso, Texas, and 55 miles southwest of Carlsbad, New Mexico. The area encompasses the southerly portion of the Guadalupe Mountains and contains the most striking and easily identifiable portion of the exposed Captain Reef, a vast formation of Permian marine limestones, recognized as one of the most extensive and significant fossilized reefs in the world.

The area abounds in wildlife, including such animals as mule deer, pronghorn, black bear, mountain lion, elk and wild turkey, but only limited hunting has been permitted by the owners of the land. Approximately 18,250 acres of the non-Federal lands within the park boundary are included in oil and gas leases, but no production has been obtained under them and present indications are that none will be obtained. The leases are for a ten year term and, in the absence of production, most of them will terminate in 1971.

The bottom end of the Guadalupe range, which resembles a huge "V," culminates at El Capitan (elevation: 8,078 feet), a sheer thousand-foot-high cliff which is visible for 50 miles or more. Guadalupe Peak, one mile to the north of El Capitan, rises to an elevation of 8,751 feet, the highest point in Texas. The escarpment running northwesterly from El Capitan magnificently exposes some 4,000 feet of Permian rock.

The Guadalupe Mountains National Park proposal would encompass 77,518 acres of which 5,632 acres in the North McKittrick Canyon area have been donated for park use by Mr. Wallace Pratt. Of the 71,886 acres remaining to be acquired, 67,312 acres are owned by Mr. J. C. Hunter. Mr. Hunter has consistently held that he would wish this unique and lovely area to be preserved for public use and has hoped that the land could be acquired by the Federal Government and established as a national park.

A Guadalupe Mountains National Park would afford visitors the opportunity to study and learn the intricacies of the ecosystems and biological forms unique to this part of the country. This is coupled with the fascinating story of the formation of the Permian reef and the aquatic origin of this desert environment, offered in a setting of rugged, pine-covered mountain grandeur—which is rare in its own right, but in this part of the country it is a situation almost incredible. Yet, here it is in this proposed national park.

Proposed Kauai National Park — Hawaii

Located on the northernmost island in the Hawaiian chain, this 97,000-acre park proposal includes the spectacular Na Pali wilderness coastline, deep valleys eroded through hundreds of colorful island-forming lava flows, the unique Alakai swamp with average precipitation measuring 500 inches annually, spectacular waterfalls, coral sand beaches and remnants of an early Hawaiian civilization.

Although formed from the successive eruptions of a shield volcano, Kauai retains little of the physical shape exhibited in the flat domes of Mauna Loa and Mauna Kea volcanoes on the Island of Hawaii. Numerous streams fed by countless tropical storms have gorged deep canyons and narrow valleys radiating from the island's ancestral volcano. Wave-formed cliffs rise like gigantic draperies along the Na Pali coast.

The national significance of the natural and scientific and historic value on Kauai has long been recognized. It was recommended by several Hawaiian residents and conservationists elsewhere that a study be made for consideration for inclusion within the National Park System. The National Park Service made a study and its preliminary professional report proposing the establishment of a Kauai National Park was released in 1965.

The proposal recommends an area of 97,000 acres. Of the total acreage, approximately 35,000 acres are in private ownership, with the remainder almost entirely under state administration. The state lands are, for the most part, under state park or forestry administration.

The major issues in opposition to the proposal concern the acquisition of private land, the prohibition against hunting in a national park, retention of water and mineral rights and commercial forestry practices. These matters are being reviewed along with public comments on the preliminary report prior to submission of recommendations to the Secretary of the Interior.

Proposed North Cascades National Park — Washington

Sometimes called the American Alps, this region of more than a million acres east of Seattle and stretching north to the Canadian border is an incomparably beautiful part of America's landscape. Rugged, towering peaks, glaciers, snow and ice fields, brilliant lakes, alpine meadows and swift rivers — such is the region of North Cascades.

The first white men who traveled into North Cascades 150 years ago were trappers and hunters. Gold and other ores were discovered sometime prior to 1850. Scattered small-scale mining operations sprang into being which, through the years, grew larger. But today mining activities are relatively unimportant in the area. The harvesting of timber began around the middle of the 19th century but it was not until decades later that commercial logging became important. Because of the abundance of high quality water, 20 water resource development projects have been built in the region since the establishment of the Gorge Power Plant in 1924.

The years since the establishment of Mount Rainier National Park in 1899 have been a time during which there were many proposals by public and private groups for additional national parks in the North Cascades area. There has been a new upsurge of interest in recent years. At the same time, as the old-growth timber on private lands adjoining the western boundary of the national forests became increasingly cut over, the dependence of the timber industry on national forests greatly increased. Thus national forest timber became a major factor in the forest products industry in the state.

As a result of these recent events, the Secretary of the Interior and the Secretary of Agriculture established a study team in 1963. Over two years later the study team issued a report which recommended a national park of 698,000 acres, including Picket Range, the Eldorado Peaks and the upper end of Lake Chelan and the Stehekin Valley. The U. S. Forest Service (which is under Department of Agriculture jurisdiction) recommended against the establishment of a national park with continued administration by the U. S. Forest Service. (National forests comprise 96 per cent of the Federal land and water acreage in the 6.3 million-acre study area which included Mount Rainier National Park.) The National Park Service recommended two national parks: One in the Glacier Peak area and another in the Mount Baker-Mount Shuksan-Picket Range area, but receded from that position in 1965, dropping the Glacier Peak proposal.

Proposed Redwood National Park — California

The inspirational qualities of virgin stands of the age-old redwood giants in natural settings have stirred men since they were first discovered. The vast redwood groves and forests constitute some of the most extraordinary scenery in the world. For 70 years conservationists have recognized the need for a Redwood National Park. The last opportunity for the establishment of such a park is probably now at hand.

The proposed Redwood National Park lies in Del Norte and Humboldt Counties, California, consisting of two separate units. The Principal Unit totals some 43,392 acres and includes the Jedediah Smith and Del Norte Coast Redwoods State Parks; lands near the Smith River north of Jed Smith; the remainder of the Mill Creek watershed; and a coastal strip south of Del Norte down to the mouth of the Klamath River. The Tall Trees Unit would be farther south on Redwood Creek in Humboldt County to preserve for public enjoyment the area where the tallest known redwoods have been found. This unit comprises some 1,400 acres, including an eight-mile access road.

In addition to outstanding features in the state parks, the Principal Unit would feature five miles of frontage on the Smith River, one of the finest clearwater salmon and steelhead rivers remaining, and provide opportunity to acquire and control the total balance of the Mill Creek watershed, including one of the major blocks of high quality still uncut redwood old growth.

In the Principal Unit, lumber companies and the state own most of the land. The Tall Trees Unit is owned by lumber companies. Lands for the Tall Trees Unit, including access, are expected to be donated. The Federal Government expects the state to donate the two state parks in the Principal Unit. The Administration proposal authorizes transfer of 31,000 acres of public lands in the King Range and the 483-acre Muir Woods National Monument to the State of California for park and recreation purposes.

Establishment of the park will pose special problems to local economy because of removal of large acreages of land from the tax rolls and the curtailment of timber cutting upon which the local economy is based. Immediate loss of $252,000 in real estate taxes to Del Norte County and 235 jobs in the timber industry are estimated. After five years, however, the stimulating effect of expanding tourist businesses should eliminate loss of county revenues and result in a net gain of 273 jobs in the area. The Administration proposal provides for annual economic adjustment payments for a five year period to county and local governmental bodies to offset the immediate impact of land acquisition.

Redwoods preservation is controversial. Various plans have been advanced by the state, the redwood industry, Sierra Club, Save-the-Redwoods League, American Forestry Association and others. The largest plan (about 97,000 acres) advanced by the Sierra Club has been sponsored by numerous bills in Congress. Basic to the controversy is the best location for the park — whether in Mill Creek or in Redwood Creek areas.

Proposed Voyageurs National Park — Minnesota

The proposed park lies about 12 miles east of International Falls, Minnesota, in St. Louis and Keechiching Counties. The northern boundary coincides with the International Boundary for about 35 miles.

This region includes a portion of the historic Voyageurs Route (voyageurs were men in the U. S. and Canada who were employed by fur traders as canoeists and guides) and possesses a wide variety of significant values. Its superlative scenery, the result of mountain building, erosion and glaciation, plus an unusually beautiful forest (see photograph, page 8) and good cover, has no counterpart in the National Park System. The combination of its human history, the ancient rock exposures of the Canadian Shield, its superb wilderness scenery, the variety of plant and animal life and the outstanding recreation opportunity makes this area one of national significance and worthy of addition to the National Park System.

The proposed park includes Kabetogama Peninsula, Kabetogama Lake and portions of Rainy and Namakan Lakes, numerous islands and lands adjacent to the lakeshores. It is in the beautiful border lake country of Minnesota, well noted for its scenic beauty and excellent boating and fishing. The island-dotted lakes surrounded by coniferous forests interspersed with deciduous trees, the beautiful bays and headlands, and the bogs and lowlands create many pleasing contrasts. The proposed area is irregular in shape, about 24 miles long from east to west, varying in width from three to fifteen miles.

The proposed park would be comprised of about 166,000 acres, including 106,000 acres of land and 60,000 acres of water. Most of the land within the proposed park is privately owned and the principal landowner is the Boise Cascade Corporation. Federal, state, county and other privately owned lands are also involved.

Considerable opposition has built up against location of the park in the Kabetogama Peninsula area. Most of the complainants are against taking additional private lands for public use and urge consideration of the Boundary Waters Canoe Area or the Grand Portage area to the east as alternate sites. The main opposition is centered in the Northland Multiple Use Association. Working for the park is the Voyageurs National Park Association.

Eldorado section (overleaf) of proposed North Cascades National Park area.